Vintage Toy Making and Toy Games for Children

By

Various Authors

A History of Toys

A toy, broadly speaking, is any item that can be used for play – generally by children and pets. Toys and games are most frequently used (consciously or not) as an enjoyable means of training the young for life in society. The young use toys and play to discover their identity, help their bodies grow strong, learn cause and effect, explore relationships, and practice skills they will need as adults. Adults use toys and play to form and strengthen social bonds, teach, reinforce lessons from their youth, discover their identity, exercise their minds and bodies, explore relationships and decorate their living spaces. Many items are designed to serve as toys (often purely as collectors' items), but goods produced for other purposes can also be used. For instance, a small child may pick up a household item and "fly" it through the air as to pretend that it is an airplane. Today, another consideration is 'interactive digital entertainment' – a wholly novel development which is quickly changing the world of toys as we know it.

The origin of toys is prehistoric; dolls representing infants, animals, and soldiers, as well as representations of tools used by adults are readily found at archaeological sites. The origin of the word "toy" is unknown, but it is believed that it was first used in the fourteenth century. Toys excavated from the Indus valley civilization (3000-1500 BCE) include small carts, whistles shaped like birds, and toy monkeys which could slide down a string. All of these earliest toys are made from materials readily found in nature, such as rocks, sticks and clay. The first 'sophisticated' toys were found in Egypt – where children played with dolls that had wigs and movable limbs which were made from stone, pottery, and wood. In Ancient Greece and Ancient Rome, children played with dolls made of wax or terracotta, sticks, bows and arrows, and yo-yos. When Greek children, especially girls, came of age it was customary for them to sacrifice the toys of their childhood to the gods. On the eve of their wedding, young girls around fourteen would offer their dolls in a temple as a rite of passage into adulthood.

Toys, of course, do not merely involve dolls and replicas; they train the brain and the body as well as the imagination. The oldest known mechanical puzzle also comes from Greece and appeared in the Third century BC, it consists of a square divided into fourteen parts, and the aim was to create different shapes from these pieces. In Iran "puzzle-locks" were made as early as the seventeenth century AD. Such examples are anomalies though, and before the enlightenment era, toys were a rarity. This changed with novel attitudes towards children; seeing them as people in and of themselves, as opposed to extensions of their household. This prompted the school of thought that children had a right to flourish and enjoy their childhood. Consequently, the variety and number of toys that were manufactured during the eighteenth century steadily rose. John Spilsbury invented the first jigsaw puzzle in 1767 to help children learn geography and the rocking horse (on bow rockers) was also developed at the same time in England, especially for the wealthy as it was thought to develop children's balance for riding real horses. The first board games were produced by John Jefferys in the 1750s, including *A Journey Through Europe*. The game was very similar to modern board games, with players moving along a track with the throw of a dice (a teetotum was actually used) and landing on different spaces would either help or hinder the player.

In the nineteenth century, the emphasis was put on toys that had an educational purpose to them, such as puzzles, books, cards and board games. Religiously themed toys were also popular, including a model Noah's Ark with miniature animals and objects from other Bible scenes. With growing prosperity among the middle class, children also had more leisure time on their hands, which led to the application of industrial methods to the manufacture of toys. More complex mechanical and optics-based toys were also invented. Carpenter and Westley began to mass-produce the kaleidoscope, invented by Sir David Brewster in 1817, and had sold over 200,000 items within three months in London and Paris. The company was also able to mass-produce magic lanterns for use in phantasmagoria and galanty shows, by developing a method of mass production using a copper plate printing process. Popular imagery on the lanterns included royalty, flora and fauna, and geographical/man-made structures from around the world.

Despite these impressive developments, the golden age of toy development was at the turn of the twentieth century. Real wages were rising steadily in the Western world, allowing even working-class families to afford toys for their children, and industrial techniques of precision engineering and mass production was able to provide the supply to meet this rising demand. Intellectual emphasis was also increasingly being placed on the importance of a wholesome and happy childhood for the future development of children. William Harbutt, an English painter, invented plasticine in 1897, and in 1900 commercial production of the material as a children's toy began. Frank Hornby was a visionary in toy development and manufacture and was responsible for the invention and production of three of the most popular lines of toys based on engineering principles in the twentieth century: Meccano, Hornby Model Railways and Dinky Toys. During the Second World War, some new types of toys were created through accidental innovation. After trying to create a replacement for synthetic rubber, the American Earl L. Warrick inadvertently invented "nutty putty" during World War II. Later, Peter Hodgson recognized the potential as a childhood plaything and packaged it as Silly Putty. In 1943, at the height of the war, Richard James was experimenting with springs as part of his military research when he saw one come loose and fall to the floor. He was intrigued by the way it flopped around on the floor – and the result became the "Slinky".

After the Second World War, as society became ever more affluent and new technology and materials (plastics) for toy manufacture became available, toys became cheap and ubiquitous in households across the Western World. Among the more well-known products of the 1950s there was the Danish company Lego's line of colourful interlocking plastic brick construction sets, Rubik's Cube, the Barbie doll and Action Man. Today there are computerized dolls that can recognize and identify objects, the voice of their owner, and choose among hundreds of pre-programmed phrases with which to respond. The materials that toys are made from have changed, what toys can do has changed, but their appeal has not. We hope the reader enjoys this book.

TOY GAMES AND TOY-MAKING.

In treating the subject of toy games adapted for in-door recreation, it should be stated at the outset that many of the manufactured and expensive toys which form the groundwork of an almost innumerable number of games are not described with any detail, because descriptions of these toys with their various uses are invariably supplied to their purchasers, and further instruction here cannot be needed. To those who can afford to procure a constant supply of new and original toys and games, no better means of learning of their appearance can be had than is supplied in the catalogues issued, for the most part gratuitously, or at a very small cost, from time to time, by the leading firms engaged in the toy trade.

As to the most simple toys, particularly those which can be made at home by the exercise of a little skill and ingenuity, and at small cost, it should always be remembered that the making of such simple toys is in itself a recreation, and affords that variety of amusement which makes recreation truly valuable. Again, there are many toys provided by the purveyors of amusements for the youngsters, which can neither be classified among toy games nor as toy-making; but it will not be altogether out of place to mention them here by way, as it were, of parenthesis. The toys more especially alluded to now are those intended to find occupation for youngsters not blessed with playmates, or who are sometimes without playmates.

There are toy bricks and toy building materials of endless descriptions and varieties. By the way, a very amusing and ingenious trick may be performed with a box of bricks familiar to all, that partakes of the simplest character. The bricks referred to are those about two inches long, an inch wide, and half an inch thick, and which are supplied in boxes containing a large quantity of bricks all of that size. If these bricks are set up on end at distances apart of about an inch and a half to an inch and three-quarters, and the one at either end gently touched, so as to fall on to the one placed next to it, the whole set will gradually fall one after the other. The bricks may be arranged serpentine fashion, winding backwards and forwards like a figure 8 or letter S; but provided the distance named is adhered to the result will be the same, and the effect of two or three hundred bricks leisurely knocking each other down will, if the figure in which they are set up be well arranged, have an almost comical appearance.

Then, again, there is the class of toys now known by the name of the originator, "Crandall's toys," all of which are made on the principle of fitting parts of the same structure together by joints. These toys are being constantly extended and made more complicated, and they afford amusement not only to those piecing them together, but also to a numerous company of on-lookers.

Among the other leading toys for in-door recreation we would mention "Noah's Arks," "Farm Yards," "Shops," "Railways," "Omnibuses," "Tram Cars," "Wagons," "Horses" (an endless delight to the very young, and which may be had in almost any form, from the simple wooden toy drawn by a handle to that now so common, and which is mounted on a miniature but well-made tricycle), animals of all sorts and noises, singing and talking birds, miniature toy musical instruments, and other toys of a never-ending variety made especially for the male portion of the juvenile population, without mentioning here, in this Boys' Book, those dolls and other toys intended for the amusement of the boys' sisters and female cousins. As an illustration of the ingenuity of the toy-producers, it may be stated that among the latest additions to the more expensive of the mechanical toys is that known as the animal album, of which we give an engraving. This book has represented on the left-hand page the figure of some animal, and on the right-hand page there is some text descriptive of the creature exhibited. On pulling a small button attached to the book, the noise or sound peculiar to the animal on the opened page will be emitted from under the opposite leaf. In the woodcut the letterpress facing the portrait of Chanticleer has been removed to show the mechanism for producing the cries of the various animals.

In short, before proceeding to the description of those toys and toy games selected for more detailed treatment, it may be observed that the possession of toys is in itself a good thing; that the making of and making use of them is better; that the capability of obtaining amusement from those owned, be they simple or be they complicated, is better still; but that it is best of all to be able also to be the means of imparting amusement to those about us.

THE ANIMAL ALBUM: A TALKING PICTURE-BOOK.

ÆOLIAN HARP.

This interesting little toy is best if made on a long box of very thin deal wood, about four or six inches deep, a circle an inch and a half in diameter, in which some small holes are to be drilled, being marked on the upper side of the box. Bridges, like the bridge of an ordinary violin or fiddle, are to be fastened on to each end of the upper side, and over these bridges are to be passed a number of strings of very fine cat-gut. The strings at one end are to be secured in the framework of the box, and at the other on screw pins, which are themselves fastened to the box. The strings can then be relaxed or tightened, as desired, by turning these pins, and the notes emitted by the different strings altered and arranged according to fancy. The instrument so made should be blown upon or placed in a current of air where the wind can pass freely over it, and then, according to the degrees of strength with which the strings are blown upon, different sounds will be produced.

ANIMATED SERPENT.

ANIMATED SERPENT.

The animated serpent is a simple and pretty toy. To make it, obtain, if possible. a piece of thin sheet copper or sheet brass, and if not, a piece of card of firm substance, but not too thick. Draw upon the material the form of a coiled-up serpent; cut out the serpent with the point of a sharp pen-knife, and fasten a thread through the tip of the tail. When this is done, fasten to the mantelpiece, or to some board to be placed thereon, the other end of the thread, taking care that the stove register is open. The weight of the serpent's body and head will cause the coils and head to fall below the suspended tail, and then, as a current of air is always passing up an open chimney, the serpent will revolve with more or less rapidity, according to the strength of the draught of air. It is well that the serpent when made should be striped green, black, and yellow, and should have glass beads, to represent eyes. Any situation in which there is a draught of air will be suitable, as well as the chimney-piece, in showing off the toy when made.

ANNULETTE.

See "Parlour Croquet."

APPLE MILL.

This is a top-toy readily made with a nut, an apple or potato, a wooden skewer, and a piece of string. First procure a good-sized Spanish or Barcelona nut, and through it bore a small hole, carefully removing all the kernel therefrom, and then make another small hole in one side of the shell. Pare down an ordinary wooden meat-skewer until it is thin enough to pass through the nut at the holes first bored therein, being careful to leave a head to the skewer at the top to prevent it passing entirely through the nut-shell. A piece of string should next be attached to the skewer at a point just beneath the head, the opposite end of which is to be passed through the hole in the side of the nut. The string is then to be wound round the skewer as the string is wound round an ordinary humming-top, leaving a small piece to pull. If an apple or potato is then stuck upon the pointed end of the skewer, and the string is pulled as when a humming-top is to be spun, the "apple mill," as made above, will spin round with considerable velocity.

APPLE WOMAN.

This is an ingenious hand-trick, and consists in so dressing up the hand as to make it represent an apple woman.

Clench the fist, holding it knuckles upwards, covering the top joint of the thumb with the top joints of the fingers. Draw on these portions of the forefinger

APPLE WOMAN.

and thumb, forming the front of the clenched fist, a face, using a few bold dots and lines to represent the eyes, eyebrows, nose, &c. Make a cap to fit the hand, and drape a pocket-handkerchief over all, fastening it as a shawl in front. The old woman so made may be made to seem to speak by slightly moving the knuckle of the thumb up and down, and to smoke by sticking a pipe between the forefinger and the thumb, the space between which joints will represent the mouth. The above illustration is a fair representation of the apple woman's face, and a careful inspection will show how the thumb and fingers are to be arranged.

BANDILOR.

This is a toy made of hard wood, and in appearance is not much unlike a pulley with a very deep groove. A piece of string is to be wound round the groove, a hole being made in the centre of the wood, through which the end of the string has first to be secured. In playing with the toy, the loose end of the string is to be held between the forefinger and thumb, and the grooved piece of wood is to be let fall. The string is thus unwound, and if the fall of the wood is suddenly checked by a sharp jerk, the Bandilor will commence to rise, and in this way may be made to continue alternately descending and ascending for a considerable time. This toy is sometimes known by the name of Quiz.

BATTLEDORE AND SHUTTLECOCK.

This is a game equally for in-door and out-door recreation, but as the mode of playing and the materials are fully described in CASSELL'S BOOK OF SPORTS AND PASTIMES, it is only necessary here to refer the reader to that work.

BELL AND HAMMER.

See "Schimmel."

BIRD WHISTLES.

Whistles to imitate the songs of birds may be readily made in different ways. Remove the spout from a small toy teapot, make a whistle at the lower end of a quill, and fit that end to the hole of the teapot left upon the spout being removed, then fill the teapot rather more than half full of water, blow the whistle, and clear bird-like notes will be sounded.

Another form of bird whistle may be made out of a piece of elder or willow. Make in the middle of a piece of either of these woods a whistle, the wood being, of course, first hollowed out. Place one end of the whistle so made in the mouth, and the opposite end just under the surface of a glass of water. By then blowing, the bird-like notes, as with the quill and the teapot, will be obtained. These whistles may be made of metal or glass as well as wood.

BIRDS, BEASTS, AND FISHES.

See "Slate Games."

BOMBARDMENT.

See "Cannonade."

BOTTLE IMPS.

BOTTLE IMPS.

Obtain from the toy-shop some small enamelled figures that are made partially hollow towards their lower part, place them in a glass jar filled quite full to the brim with water, and carefully close the jar by covering it tightly with a piece of parchment. Now, by alternately placing the hand upon the cover and lifting it off again, the figures are made to descend and ascend in the water. This is caused by the hollowness before mentioned, the cavities in the figures retaining a certain quantity of air, and imparting the requisite buoyancy to them. When the hand is pressed upon the parchment cover of the bottle the water rises, in consequence of the pressure, into the figures. The air so being compressed into less space, renders the imps less buoyant, and they fall; on the pressure being removed they rise again.

BROTHER JONATHAN.

This is a game of American origin, and consists in pitching a copper or some other convenient object at the spaces of a diagram arranged and numbered, as shown in the accompanying plan. The larger spaces should bear the smaller numbers, and the smaller spaces the larger numbers. A mark from which the pitch is to be made must be arranged, and those pitches only count which are made into one or other of the compartments; pitches made upon the different lines are not counted. The number marked in the compartment pitched into counts towards game, which may be fixed at any number according to the pleasure of the players.

20	3		4
II	20	10	
2	7		9
20		1	20
6	8		5

BROTHER JONATHAN.

Crack Loo is a somewhat similar game, and it consists in pitching on a boarded floor with the object of pitching on one or other of the cracks separating the boards.

CAMERA (MINIATURE).

The materials required to make this toy are a small pill-box, a small piece of broken looking-glass about half an inch square, and a little piece of beeswax. Bore a small hole in the centre of the lid of the pill-box, and another hole in the side of the box; then, by means of the beeswax, stick the bit of looking-glass across the bottom of the box, at an angle of forty-five degrees. By looking now through one of the holes in the box the reflection of objects passing behind will be seen. In making a miniature camera it is not necessary that the materials used should be so small as those here set forth, but even of such materials as those mentioned an effective little toy may be easily constructed, and more ambitious cameras are to be made on just the same principle.

CANNONADE.

The game of Cannonade, or Castle Bagatelle as it is more generally called, is a capital Round Game. The rules for playing it, which are supplied with the board and other apparatus, are somewhat intricate, and the toy is too elaborate to be made except at a manufactory. A number of miniature castles, enclosed in miniature fortresses, are arranged inside and around the edge of a circular tray board; a number of well-turned balls, equal to the number of castles being played, are then placed tolerably near each other towards the middle of the board, and among the balls so placed each player alternately spins as vehemently as possible a good-sized teetotum; the teetotum sends the balls flying among the castles, and the owners of the castles overturned pay forfeit to the spinner of the teetotum, while the owners of the castles that remain standing receive forfeit from him.

CANNONADE, OR CASTLE BAGATELLE.

There is a version of this game known at the toy-shops as the " Game of Bombardment." It is a German introduction, and although not so good a game as that of Castle Bagatelle, is very similar in principle, affords good fun to a round party, and is not quite so expensive to purchase as the older English toy.

CARPET CROQUET.

See " Parlour Croquet."

CASTLE BAGATELLE.

See " Cannonade."

COMMON WHISTLE.

But little description either of the Common Whistle, or of how to make it, is necessary, it being so well known. The tin whistle can hardly be made except with the aid of expensive tools, but it may be purchased at a very trifling cost. No lad, however, need be without a whistle even when no toy-shop is near. A good whistle may be made out of almost any straight piece of scooped-out wood, the model of the tin whistle being adhered to as closely as possible. A nice piece of elder neatly carved and plugged may even be made to do duty for a miniature flute, and so made, various notes are to be extracted from it.

CRACK LOO.

See " Brother Jonathan."

CUP AND BALL.

The Cup and Ball has long been a favourite toy. It consists of a stem of ivory or some hard wood, one end of which is pointed, while to the other is fixed a small shallow cup, To the stem an ivory or hard wood ball is attached by means of a piece of string, and in one side of the ball a hole is drilled into which the pointed end of the stem fits. The game is, when the ball is loosely attached to the stem, to throw it up so as to catch it either within the cup at the one end of the stem, or on the point at the other end, the latter feat being by far the most difficult. To accomplish this, the stem is to be held lightly in the right hand; then make the ball revolve by twirling it between the thumb and forefinger of the left hand, and when its motion becomes steady, throw it up with a slight jerk of the right wrist, and as it descends endeavour to catch it in one of the ways just mentioned. Calculate well the length of the string in throwing up the ball, so that it is not thrown to the full length of the string, or it will be almost impossible to succeed in catching it.

CUPOLETTE.

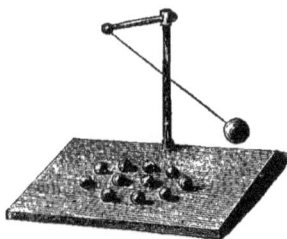

Although its warmest admirers will hardly maintain that the game of Cupolette requires much skill, yet it succeeds in affording considerable amusement. The materials for the game are a board with a number of sunken and differently numbered cups, a ball for each cup, and a movable arm, which is attached to the board, and from which a ball, heavier than the other balls, is suspended by a cord. The play commences with the balls placed in the cups ; the first player then turns the arm to any

CUPOLETTE.

position he prefers, draws the suspended ball out to the full length of its cord, and allows it to swing back, so as to strike one or more of the balls out of the cups. Each ball knocked out scores one point ; a ball struck out of one cup and into another scores the number of points indicated by the number of the cup; a ball struck off the board is lost and scores nothing. Each player is entitled to four strokes, and each player, as it becomes his turn to play, replaces all the balls as at first, and proceeds as above. A game is usually either sixty-one or a hundred and one, according to the number of players. Sides may be formed if it is desired.

CUT-WATER.

The toy known as the Cut-Water is made in the following manner:—Cut a circular piece of tin or sheet-lead, three inches or so in diameter, into the form of a circular saw; bore two holes in it along the diameter at about an inch apart; through these holes pass the two ends of a string, tie the ends of the string together, and the toy is made. To use it, the string is to be taken up in the two hands, the metal saw being allowed to hang loosely at the middle of the string, and then thrown round and round until the string becomes very tightly twisted.

CUT-WATER.

Upon the hands then being drawn outwards, the string untwists, and the metal saw rapidly revolves. So soon as the string is all untwisted, the hands should be allowed to go slightly nearer each other, when it will be found that the Cut-Water will revolve in the opposite direction. Again, when the string has become once more twisted, the hands should be drawn outwards, then inwards, and again outwards, and so on alternately. The name of "Cut-Water" is derived from a common way of playing with the toy. It is dipped a little below the surface of water whilst being spun, and it then sends showers of spray towards the player who spins it, or away from him, according to the direction in which it may be spinning.

An imitation Cut-Water may be more readily, and indeed often is, made by passing a piece of string through two of the holes of a common breeches' button, and treating the toy so made as explained above.

DANCING HIGHLANDER.

The Dancing Highlander, like the Apple Woman and a few other imitations described among the toy games, is really a hand performance supplemented by a few accessories. For the performance of the Dancing Highlander, get an old glove and cut off the tops of the first two fingers down to about the second joint; next will be required a very small pair of baby's socks, which are to be painted some plaid pattern, and fitted to the first and second fingers. Draw on the glove, then pull the socks on the first two fingers, padding out that for the first finger so as to be equal in length to that for the second. The figure of a Highlander in his national costume, which should have been first prepared out of cardboard and appropriately coloured, is then to be pasted on to the back of the glove; the tops of the two first fingers of the gloves should do duty for shoes, and the uncovered portions of the performer's fingers will show as the bare knees of the kilted Scot, who may then be made to dance or perform any of those wild antics usually attributed to the Highlander when his foot is on his native heath.

DANCING PEA.

A common pea, two small pins, and a piece of the straight stem of a broken clay tobacco-pipe, are the requirements for making this curious little toy. Run the pins crosswise through the pea, and cover their points with a little bit of sealing-wax, to prevent mischief in the event of the pins striking any one's face. Put the point of one of the pins down the stem of the tobacco-pipe, so that the pea will rest thereon. Place the other end of the pipe in the mouth, holding the head back and the pipe stem perpendicularly. Upon then blowing steadily the pea will dance amusingly in the air.

DART AND TARGET.

The apparatus required for this game is easily made. The dart is a straight piece of stick, about six inches long, with a pin stuck in at one end, and a paper guide at the other. The pin, which should be an ordinary large-sized pin, must have the head removed, and be pushed into the end of the stick, with the point outwards, and then secured in its place by a piece of twine or sealing-wax. The guide is made of a square piece of paper folded twice from corner to corner, and then inserted in cross slits made at the opposite end of the stick. The target is best if made of a piece of soft wood board, and should have painted on it three or four concentric circles of different colours, with a bull's-eye in the centre. The darts should then be thrown at the target from some distance to be agreed upon, and scores made according to the nearness of the darts to the bull's-eye. Each circle should be differently numbered, the outer circle counting one, the next two, and so on, an extra allowance being made for the bull's-eye.

DARTELLE.

This is the name given to Dart and Target at the toy shops. It makes a pretty toy, and combines in itself both darts and duly marked target, with the necessary instructions for play.

DECIMAL GAME.

Get a long piece of board and fix into it ten pins in a row. On each pin place a ring, and the game then is to make the ten rings into five pairs of rings in five moves, passing over two occupied pins with every move. The feat is to be accomplished in the following among other methods:

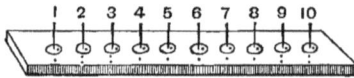
DECIMAL GAME.

Let the accompanying diagram represent the pins, board, and the rings as first placed thereon ; remove No. 7 to No. 10, No. 6 to No. 3, No. 4 to No. 9, No. 8 to No. 2, and No. 1 to No. 5. The changes may be done in the reverse way, by commencing from No. 4 to No. 1, instead of No. 7 to No. 10, and so on, and other slight variations may be introduced. The game may also be played with ten counters, or ten pieces of paper, on a table or board, and without any pins. Indeed, children are frequently seen playing the game out of doors with ten common stones.

DEMON BOTTLE.

Cut a piece of pith of wood, or some equally light substance, into the shape of a small bottle, and at its base fasten the half of a small bullet (*a, see* figure). Down the centre of the bottle bore a hole, and fit the hole with a steel pin (*a b*). The bottle so made may be rendered obedient to the commands of its owner, who, when he wishes it to stand upright and resist the commands of the bystanders, will previously have removed the pin; when he wishes it to act in the contrary manner he will insert the pin, which will be found to counteract the weight of the

DEMON BOTTLE.

bullet, and the bottle will obediently recline after receiving its owner's orders to do so; the owner of course then being careful to give such orders.

DRAWING-ROOM ARCHERY.

See " Puff and Dart," " Dart and Target," and " Dartelle."

DUTCH RACQUETS.

Dutch Racquets, or the Dutch Top Game, is very similar to the game of Castle Bagatelle, or Cannonade. The appliances needed are somewhat expensive, and the description of how to play the game, with the rules by which it is governed, is supplied with the toy.

The game is played on a board fitted with metal barriers that are variously numbered, and on the different numbers miniature skittles are placed. A metal top is then spun at one end of the board, and as it travels, the skittles, or some of them, will be overthrown. The numbers covered by the skittles overthrown count towards game.

ENFIELD SKITTLES.

This is a game played on a level board with raised edges. Nine small wooden pins are arranged at one end of the board as skittles are arranged in the ordinary skittle-alley game. These skittle pins are then bowled at by means of a small ivory or boxwood ball, propelled with an ordinary billiard cue. The game is frequently arranged for on an ordinary dining-room table, precautions being first taken to prevent the ball from rolling off.

FLYING CONES.

Flying Cones are made of hard wood, hollow, a hole being made at one side so as to produce a humming sound when the completed toy is being spun. Two such cones are fastened together at the apex. The spinning apparatus consists of two thin sticks, to the tips of which a string of about a yard long has to be tied. To play the toy, lay the cones on some flat surface, take one of the sticks in each hand, holding them at the opposite ends to those to which the string has been attached, slip the string under the cones, so as to catch them just at that point where they have been united, being careful that the toy is somewhat

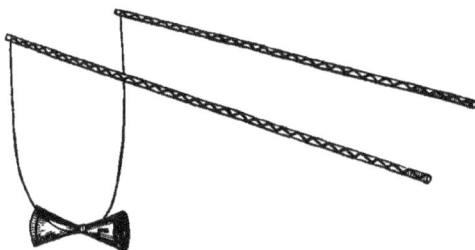

FLYING CONES.

nearer to the right-hand than to the left-hand stick. Next, raise the sticks, at the same time making such a movement with the right hand as to set the double cone revolving on the string. By a sort of whipping movement, first with one hand and then with the other, it may be kept spinning; when quickly spun, it will make a humming sound, and with practice considerable dexterity in the use of this toy will be easily attained.

When the toy has obtained sufficient speed to commence humming, many pretty feats may be shown with it. It may be flung in the air, and as it falls it may be caught on the loose or tightened string, or on one of the sticks, and made to roll towards one or other of the hands of the player. Two players, each being provided with the necessary sticks, with string attached, may keep a flying cone spinning a long time, and at the same time be continually throwing it backwards and forwards from one to the other. This toy is also known as Le Diable, and is usually sold in the toy-shops under that name.

FRENCH AND ENGLISH.

See " Slate Games."

GAS BALLOONS.

Small Gas Balloons are made of thin sheet india-rubber or gutta-percha, or tissue paper; larger ones are made of oiled silk. Cut gores of the material to be used sufficient in number when fastened together, the sides of each gore overlapping the gore fastened to it, to form a globe of the desired size with pear-shaped ends. Join the gores together, so as to make them completely air-tight; when the heavier materials are used they should be sewn together, and then covered with glue or thin varnish. At the lower end of the balloon insert a tube, and tie all the narrow tips of the gores firmly round it. Cover all with a solution made of india-rubber dissolved in naphtha and turpentine, and over the balloon place a net bag that has been previously made of the proper size and shape.

The gas with which the balloon is to be filled is made in the following manner:—Put a pound of granulated zinc or iron filings into two quarts of water in a stone jar, and add gradually a pint of sulphuric acid. Have a tube of glass or metal run through the bung with which the jar is corked, and after taking the materials out of doors, fill the balloon by connecting this tube with the tube already placed at its mouth. When the balloon is filled, tie its neck very tightly, and it will rise into the air. Common coal-gas may be used when it can be obtained. A small car made of some light material may be attached to the netting which goes over the balloon.

Soap-bubbles inflated with gas may be made in the following manner:— Fill a bladder with hydrogen gas, adapt a tobacco-pipe to the mouth of the bladder, and dip the bowl of the pipe into soap and water; then press the bladder, and bubbles will be duly formed, which floating away will at once rise in the air.

Toy balloons ready to be filled with hydrogen gas may be now purchased at many toy-shops, or of philosophical instrument-makers.

GERMAN BALLS.

Luck and skill combined in about equal degrees make the principal charm of this game, which is a very simple one, and which in many respects resembles the game of marbles known as " Die Shot."

The game may be played equally well in-doors on a carpeted floor or out of doors on a lawn, or any other level surface. The materials required are a number of balls, and a larger ball shaped as a die with eight sides, numbered respectively 1, 2, 3, 4, 5, 6, 7, and 8. The die is placed on the ground with the figure 8 downwards, and the players, each being supplied with a ball, bowl alternately at the die from some point at a distance from the die to be agreed upon. If the die is missed, nothing is scored, and in some places the player who misses pays one to a pool. If the die is hit, the player whose ball hit it scores the number on the side of the die which remains uppermost.

Under some rules each player puts a stake into a pool, and he who attains the highest score in a certain number of throws wins the pool. If, however, any player should succeed in turning the die so that the number 8 remains uppermost, he takes the pool at once, and a new game is then commenced.

GERMAN BILLIARDS.

This is a game played with balls on a board on which is a complicated arrangement of pins, hoops, holes, recesses, and cups, the holes, recesses, and cups in which are variously numbered. The balls are propelled by means of a spring fitted into one side of the board, and the scores are in accordance with the numbers marked in the respective holes, recesses, and cups that the balls fall into after wandering through the many pins and hoops that are fixed all over the board.

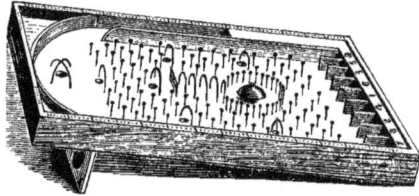

GERMAN BILLIARDS.

HAT MEASUREMENT.

The practice known as Hat Measurement has sprung up owing to the fact that very few people either have but very little idea of the probable height of very common objects, or if they know the actual height in inches of those objects, are unable to demonstrate that height. The judgment is very frequently tested by asking the company present to mark on a wall about the height of an ordinary chimney-pot hat; and in the majority of cases, upon a hat being actually brought in, it will be found that the height marked is sufficient for at least a hat and a half.

HOMEWARD BOUND.

See "Patchesi."

HYDRAULIC DANCER.

Make a little figure out of a piece of cork, pith, or some equally light material; place in the figure a small hollow cone of thin leaf brass; then set the figure on any water-jet or small fountain, and it will remain suspended on the top of the water, and will jump, dance, and move about in a very amusing manner. A hollow ball of thin copper, placed on a jet or fountain in a similar way, will remain suspended, turning round and spreading the water gracefully about it.

IMMOVABLE CARD.

Upon the face of it, and on first thoughts, it would appear to be the easiest possible thing to blow over an ordinary visiting card placed on a table, provided it be not secured in any mechanical manner. If a visiting card is neatly turned down at the narrow edges, about a quarter or a third of an inch, so that the edges turned down are at right-angles with the remainder of the card, and the card be then placed on the turned down edges, the feat would seem to be still more easy than if the card were simply placed flat on the table. The contrary, however, is the case, and unless let into the secret one may blow at a card so placed for hours without being able to overturn it.

To accomplish the feat, the blowing must be done on the table, not on the card, and at some distance from the card.

INDIAN SKITTLE POOL.

See "Skittle Cannonade."

JACK-IN-THE-BOX.

The toy known as Jack-in-the-Box is familiar to all, and is always the source of much fun; it may be readily made by any ingenious lad who will carefully follow the accompanying description :—

The toy consists of a box containing a figure of some comical shape. Inside the figure a piece of wire, known as the spring, is coiled up, corkscrew-wise, like the spring within a carriage candle lamp. The box should be made so that when the lid is closed the wire or spring within the figure is compressed; on the removal of the pressure from the lid the wire regains its original form, and out springs the figure. The figure is sometimes secured to the bottom of the box, and sometimes attached to the side by a long piece of string, and then when the lid is suddenly unfastened, Jack will spring out of his hiding-place and fly up high into the air.

JAPANESE FAN.

See " Magic Fan."

JERK STRAWS.

This is a rough version of the game of Spillikins, or Spelicans, more fully described further on. Jerk-straws, Jack-straws, or Juggling-sticks, as they are indifferently called, are a number of small rounded sticks, forty or fifty or more, about twice as long and of the same thickness as a common Tandstickor match. These are thrown loosely in a confused heap upon the table, and the players have to remove them, one by one, by means of a longer stick, hooked or pointed as desired, without, in the process of removing one stick, touching or disturbing any other. The first player removes as many as he can in this way, but as soon as he disturbs any other than the one to be removed, in the slightest degree, or touches any other one, he gives place to the next player, and so on. At the end of the game, the player has won who has secured the largest number of sticks.

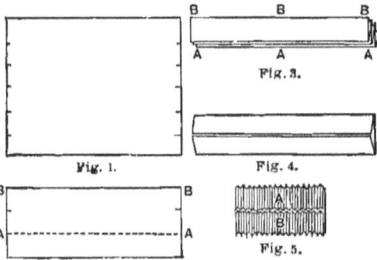

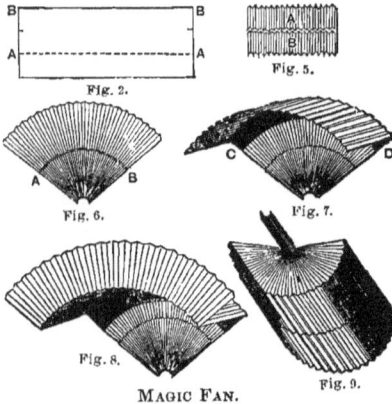

Fig. 1.

Fig. 2.

Fig. 3.

Fig. 4.

Fig. 5.

Fig. 6.

Fig. 7.

Fig. 8.

Fig. 9.

MAGIC FAN.

LE DIABLE.

See " Flying Cones."

MAGIC FAN.

The description of several paper toys appears in this section of the book, but of them all the Magic Fan is the most ingenious, its varieties being so numerous. It is known by the names of the " Magic Fan," " Japanese Fan," " Puzzle-Wit," and " Trouble-Wit," and is often exhibited for profit in the public streets of populous places by members of that class of people who prefer living by their wits to working hard. As a toy, however, to be made at home, it is well worth something more than a mere superficial acquaintanceship.

In its manufacture a piece of good stout paper will be required, in size twenty-four inches by nineteen, or proportionately larger or smaller. The paper is to be measured into six equal parts, the divisions being marked on the margin, as shown in Fig. 1. Double the paper in half, as shown in Fig. 2. Fold the uppermost half outwards, making the fold as shown in the same figure by the letters A A. Turn the paper over and fold the other half in precisely the same way, thus making the paper as shown in Fig. 3. Upon examining the edge A A A, two openings between the folds will be seen, whereas at the edge B B B, three openings will be found. The hand has next to be inserted into the middle of these latter openings, and the paper folded outwards to the right and left, and turned over, when it will show as in Fig. 4. Then pinch the paper from end to end in plaits like a ruff, three-eighths of an inch in depth, so that when it is all pinched it will be in small compass, as in the Fig. 5. The Magic Fan is then complete, and all that remains is to learn how to produce its variety of shapes. It is said that as many as from sixty to seventy varieties have been produced; a few only will, however, be here indicated, as by attention to the directions now given it will be a comparatively easy matter to ring the changes on the kinds specified. It must always be remembered that every time the form of the fan is changed, the paper must be again well pinched together, in order that the folds of the plaits may remain plainly and strongly marked. Unless the folds are kept in order the fan cannot be properly worked.

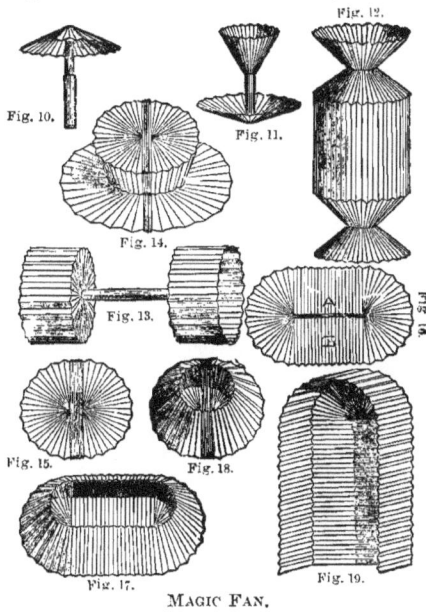

MAGIC FAN.

To produce the first form, the common-shaped fan, Fig. 6, catch the folded paper, Fig. 5, at the bottom with both hands, pinch it in and then spread out the top. For Fig. 7, insert the fingers at A and pass them round to B, raising the paper. To turn Fig. 7 into Fig. 8, insert the fingers at C and pass them round to D.

For the next change, catch the paper by the part now uppermost, pinch that part well together, and the paper takes the form of a scoop (Fig. 9), the upper part of the fan, Fig. 8, becoming the handle of the scoop. Pinch the paper again into the form of Fig. 5, lift up the upper part A, bring the lower plaits, B, well together, and with one hand arrange the upper part, so as to form the head of a mushroom (Fig. 10). A new form may be got by raising part of the double head of the mushroom. For Fig. 11, reverse the paper and spread out the lower part, so that it may represent the body of a wine-glass, that which in Fig. 10 was the head of the mushroom will soon appear as the foot of the glass. To make the Chinese lantern, Fig. 12, open out all the paper and twist it round; catch it now by the central part, and by compressing the central folds well together, something like two of the enormous wheels of a steam stone-crusher will be produced (Fig. 13). The butter cooler, Fig. 14, is obtained by opening the paper out again and catching it at the two ends.

The original form, Fig. 5, must then be again reverted to, and a fresh start may be made by catching the paper at both ends and folding it so as to represent Fig. 15. By drawing it out the table mat. Fig. 16, will next be shown. Raise up the paper at the letters A and B of Fig. 16, and there will appear a dish in the form of Fig. 17. Fig. 18 is obtained by then pressing the paper inwards. The sentry box, Fig. 19, comes by drawing the paper out, and letting it loose at the foot. And so on, many shapes not here set forth may be obtained.

Experiment freely on the Magic Fan; if spoiled it costs nothing but a little patience and a few minutes of time to re-make, and a dexterous lad will produce staircases, sofas, chairs, flower-pots, windows and window-blinds, nightcaps, boxes, &c. &c. &c.

MAGIC FIGURE.

This is an amusing and easily made toy. Its peculiarity lies in this, that however it may be knocked about, so long as it remains whole, it rises of its own accord to its feet and retains its balance with a gently swaying motion. The figure should be cut out of cork or pith, or something equally light, and may be clothed by gumming on to it some silk floss or other similar substance; to its base, but hidden as much as possible, should be fastened the half of a leaden bullet, with the semi-circular side undermost. The weight of the pedestal will then be sufficient to secure the recovery of the figure immediately after being made to lie prostrate.

MAGIC FIGURE.

It will be seen by reference that the principle underlying the manufacture of this toy is similar to that of the Demon Bottle, previously described, the variation being the steel pin in the bottle which, when inserted, counteracts the effect of the weight adjusted to the base of the figure.

MAGIC FLUTE.

The magic flute is to be made out of a good sound and unused cork, which has in it neither holes nor cracks. Place the cork against the teeth, holding it tightly between the lips, and play upon it with the handles of two prongs or forks or the bowls of two spoons. An imitation of the piccolo or small flute will thus be produced, and almost any simple quick air may be played upon it.

MAGICIAN OF MOROCCO.

The Magician of Morocco is a hand performance similar in character to those described under the headings of the Apple Woman and the Dancing Highlander. He is made (*see* Fig. 1) by holding up a hand, bending down the fourth and little fingers, placing the thumb in front, holding the first finger straight up, and the middle finger slanting half-way between the first and fourth fingers. The top joint of the first finger is to be dotted to represent a face.

Fig. 1.—SKELETON OF THE MAGICIAN.

and on the tip of the finger a handkerchief, knotted at one corner to represent a cap, is to be placed, the remainder of the handkerchief being draped about the hand to do duty for the robe (*see* Fig. 2). This robe looks more effective if the handkerchief out of which it is made is of some bright colour or colours; an Indian silk handkerchief makes both a capital robe and cap combined; the cap may, indeed, then be easily made to look very like an ordinary Turkish fez.

It will thus be seen that while the first finger in the hand does duty for head, shoulders, and bust, the middle finger, when the whole figure is held sideways to the company, shows as the arms, and the body is made full by means of the position of the thumb and other two fingers.

It is necessary that the Magician of Morocco should have some long outlandish name, and to ensure his success that he should be very voluble with quackeries, divinations, tricks, jests, prophecies, conundrums, scandals, and nonsense of every sort and description; his conversation being accompanied by judicious nods and twists of the head, as it will not be easy to impart much of a twinkle to his eyes.

MAGNETIC SWAN.

The Magnetic Swan, and other articles made in the same manner, will illustrate the properties of the Magnetic Wand. A number of such articles, to represent swans, ducks, small boats, &c., may be made and placed in a basin or tub of water, and kept in motion by a judicious use of the wand. Be careful to model the articles so that they may undoubtedly represent those objects they are intended to resemble.

Fig. 2.—THE MAGICIAN OF MOROCCO.

Swans, ducks, boats, and such birds and things as swim or float on the surface of water, should be made out of cork, pith, or light wood, with a small piece of magnetised steel run through the body. Swans should be covered with white wax, thinly spread over the body of the bird, and the ducks and boats should be treated in the same way, with the addition of being properly coloured afterwards. Glass beads for eyes may be placed in the heads of the birds. Some care in balancing and loading these objects will have to be taken to ensure them floating properly and steadily.

Fish may also be made in a similar way, but much nicety has to be shown to load them so as to sink them below the surface of the water, and yet to make them sufficiently buoyant to keep them from sinking to the bottom.

Toys of this nature are supplied at a small cost at most toy-shops.

MAGNETIC WAND.

A number of very pleasing experiments may be performed by means of the Magnetic Wand. It is made out of a rod of hard wood, about ten inches long by a third of an inch thick. A hole is to be drilled into this rod, and in the hole is to be placed a strongly magnetised steel wire. Two small knobs should then be placed upon the reverse ends of the wand, and, in order that it may be readily known at which end of the wand is the attractive and at which end the repellent point of the magnetised wire, the knobs ought either to be differently carved or one or both of them should bear some distinctive mark. The letters N and S are suitable as specifying the north and the south poles, by which terms the opposite ends of the magnetised wire are scientifically expressed. The wand so made is complete, and by holding one or other of its ends to the tips of small articles floating in water, made after the manner described in

the manufacture of the Magnetic Swan, such articles may be made to either follow after or swim from the wand according as it is the north or the south pole which is held out.

It is an easy matter to magnetise a bit of steel wire, and under this heading of how to make a Magnetic Wand, a few hints on magnetising common objects of steel and iron will not be out of place.

An ordinary poker may be magnetised in a very simple manner. Hold it in the left hand, pointing it somewhat inclined from the perpendicular, so that the lower end is towards the north, then strike the poker several times smartly with a large iron hammer, and to a slight extent it will then be found to possess the powers of a magnet. Another method is as follows:—Get an old large iron poker, and a similar pair of tongs, such as may be found forming a part of the set of fire-irons formerly supplied for kitchen use. Fix the poker upright, and hold to it a bar about three inches long of soft steel, which should be about a quarter of an inch broad, but not more than a twentieth of an inch in thickness. Make on one end of the steel a mark, and let that end be held downwards. The steel should not be held to the poker with the hand, but should be suspended on a piece of silk held in the left hand, and so suspended as to touch the poker. Then grasp the tongs a little below the middle with the right hand, and keeping them as nearly vertical as possible, rub the steel bar with the lower end of the tongs, from the marked end of the bar to its upper end about ten times on each side of it. By this means the bar will receive enough magnetism to enable it to lift at the marked end a small steel key. Or if the bar so magnetised be suspended at its centre, and made to rest on a point, the marked end will turn to the north.

Steel fire-irons which have remained untouched during the summer period, and have at the same time remained resting on the fender, in an ordinary living-room, will be found after a few months to have become possessed of magnetic properties.

A common sewing needle is readily magnetised by passing, when gently pressed against it, the north pole of a magnet from the eye to the point of the needle. After the end of the needle has been reached, the magnet must not be passed back along it again to the eye, or the effect will be destroyed; but the effect is increased if the magnet is passed several times in succession from the eye to the point. A needle so magnetised may be used in the place of the magnetised wire required for a small Magnetic Wand.

MAGNIFYING PINHOLE.

See " Microscope (Toy)."

MECHANICAL BUCEPHALUS.

See " Pegasus in Flight."

MICROSCOPE (TOY).

Toy microscopes, or miniature microscopes that may be easily made, are of two sorts. The first and simplest is sometimes called the Magnifying Pinhole. Take a blackened card, and make a hole in it with the point of a fine needle. Hold up the card, and look through the hole so made at any small object held at about an inch from the card, and the object so held will appear magnified about ten times. Remove the card from the eye, leaving the object looked at in its former position, and it will then not be seen at all; this is accounted for from the well-known quality of the eye that it is unable unaided to discover a single object not more than an inch away.

Another sort of toy microscope is made out of a thin plate of lead or brass. Bore a hole in it with a fine awl or a large needle, and let a drop of clear water fall into the hole so as to fill it up completely. Then place any object that it is wished to examine below the thin plate, and immediately below the globule of water. Look through the globule, and the object looked at will be seen, apparently magnified about a hundred and fifty times. A full water-bottle also has microscopic powers.

MOCKING CALL.

The Mocking Call is a little instrument by which one may imitate the song of birds, animals, and various other sounds, and is to be made in the following manner :—Cut a small square piece from the green leaf of a common leek, lay it on a table or clean board, and with great care scrape away a piece of the green pulpy substance of the leaf, being very careful on no account to injure the fine outer skin. Place the instrument so made in the roof of the mouth, with that side downwards on which is the outer skin. Press the instrument gently with the tongue into its place, and then blow between the tongue and the upper teeth. At first sounds will be emitted that will not readily be recognised as similar to those of birds or animals, but with practice and patience the barking of a dog, the neighing of a horse, or the notes of many of the song birds, may be successfully imitated. When the Mocking Call is not in use, it should be kept moist by placing it in a glass of water. This toy is useful when used in a ventriloquial entertainment.

MOORISH FORT.

The game of Moorish Fort is a good round game of skill. It is a comparatively new game, and is supplied by the toy-dealers, with rules, at a reasonable price; but as the materials to play the game with may be found in any tolerably extensive collection of toys if supplemented by a fort and a few rods, which can easily be made, some readers of this book may, if unable to purchase the materials, feel inclined to practise their ingenuity in adapting the toys they possess to play the game.

Fig. 1.—THE FORT.

A round fort, constructed in the manner shown in the accompanying woodcut (Fig. 1), is placed in the centre of an ordinary dining- room table. The players should number six or less, and be divided into two sides, each side taking opposite positions; each player should

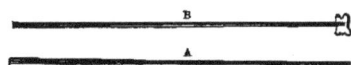

Fig. 2.—CUE (A) AND REST (B).

be provided with a small round ball (those supplied with nine-pins do admirably), and the player, armed with a cue about eighteen inches to two feet long (Fig. 2, A), should strike his ball towards the fort. A rest for the cue (Fig. 2, B), with x-piece at the end, of the same length as the cue should also be supplied, to facilitate the striking of the ball when at a distance from the player, as it is to be made a rule that no player may, when playing, place his hands or arms on the table. That side which first gets all its balls into the fort wins, but a code of rules may be drafted embodying these and other regulations at the pleasure of the players.

NAVETTE.

NAVETTE.

The game of Navette is played with a bridge having numerous arches, each one of which bears a distinctive number, higher or lower, according to the size of the arch and the difficulty of attaining the object of the game, which is bowling discs, or small balls, at the bridge when placed on the floor or on the table, so that the balls may pass under one or other of the arches of the bridge. The players bowl alternately at the bridge, and he who makes the highest score in an agreed number of bowls of the ball wins. The arch-board used in marble games may be utilised for this game.

NINE PINS.

The toy-box containing Nine Pins, for playing the game of that name, together with the requisite number of balls, is to be purchased for a very trifling sum. Inasmuch as both pins and balls have to be turned in a lathe, it is almost impossible for any lad with an ordinary chest of tools to make them for himself, and, indeed, the game of Nine Pins is not a game usually played at by lads of an age able to make their own toys—it is a very small child's game. The game is played in two ways, either by throwing or bowling the balls at the pins, or by attaching a ball to a rope or string suspended from the ceiling, and so swinging the ball at the pins.

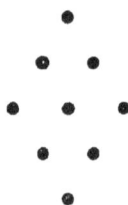

PLAN OF NINE PINS.

The pins may be set up in any manner agreeable to the players, either in a line, circle, or in the same way as in the game of skittles, in the form shown in the diagram. The number of pins knocked down counts towards game, and the player who can knock all down in the fewest throws or swings of the ball wins.

NOUGHTS AND CROSSES.

See " Slate Games."

OBEDIENT SOLDIER.

A toy similar in principle to the Demon Bottle, previously described, is the toy known as the Obedient Soldier. He should be made of pith, cork, or some very light wood, should be carved with a soldier's busby and tunic, and have in his arms a rifle at the "shoulder arms" position. The barrel of the rifle must be made hollow, in order that in it may be placed, when desired, a piece of solid steel wire. The whole figure is to be fastened at the feet on to the flat side of the half of a leaden bullet. Upon the steel wire being inserted in the barrel of the rifle, the soldier will lie down, and upon its being removed he will stand upright. The secret of these actions should rest with the performer who shows off the ways of the Obedient Soldier, and it will be necessary, in order to preserve this secrecy, that some dexterity be exhibited in the placing or removing of the steel wire.

PALADA.

The game of Palada is a game very much resembling that of Cup and Ball, and has become quite a popular amusement. The toy consists of a slim and tapering rod, the thick end of which is used as the handle, and at the opposite end is a piece of cane bent into an oval form. Attached to the rod, and at about a foot or a foot and a half from the oval end, a solid egg-shaped substance is fastened by a piece of string half as long again as the distance from the oval end towards which it is secured.

OBEDIENT
SOLDIER.

The object of the game is to catch the egg-shaped substance on the oval end of the rod, which is made large enough to allow of the egg finding a secure resting-place, but at the same time smaller than the egg, so that it may not fall through.

PALADA.

PAPER TOYS.

A very considerable number of toys may be constructed out of paper alone, and much amusement may be obtained in the making of such toys, as well as from the uses to which they can be put when made. The Magic Fan and kindred objects have been explained under that heading, and the following are a few other objects that, with a little practice, it will be found very easy for any one to make at pleasure.

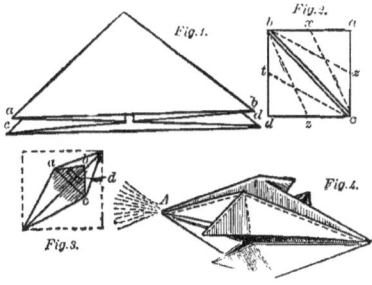

Paper Bellows.—The first in the alphabetical list of paper toys is that known as paper bellows, and a very good imitation of a pair of bellows it will be found to be.

Get a piece of paper of the substance of an ordinary sheet of note-paper, cut it into a square each side of which is at least twelve inches long, and fold it double, by making two of the corners meet with the middle line stretching between the other two corners. Open the paper out and fold it again, by making the other two corners meet, and upon it being again opened out, the folds will be left in the shape of a St. Andrew's Cross. Turn the paper over, and holding two of the folds between the finger and thumb of each hand, press them inward, and press the paper quite flat, so as to make it take the form shown in Fig. 1. Make the corners *a* and *b* meet at *e*; turn the paper over, and make the corners *c* and *d* also meet at the same point *e*. Turn the first side uppermost again, and the paper will show as in Fig. 2. Make creases in the paper, by folding *a* to *b*, *a* to *c*, *d* to *b*, and *d* to *c*; the creases should then show as indicated by the dotted lines in the figure, the paper being folded out immediately after each inward fold. Next pinch together between the finger and thumb those parts indicated by the letters *a*, *x*, *z* and *d*, *w*, *y*; pinch first the one, and then the other, and the paper will fall naturally into the form given by the folds, and will appear like Fig. 3; the dotted lines outside the figure representing the reverse side of the paper, the letters *a*, *b*, *c* forming the handle of one side of the bellows. Afterwards turn the paper over, and do with the other side as last described, by first folding the paper and then pinching it into shape; the handle of the other side of the bellows will so be formed, and the toy is complete, as represented by Fig. 4. The bellows are blown by alternately pulling out the paper by the handles and closing it again quickly, when wind will be found coming out of the bellows at the point marked *A*.

Paper Boat.—For this toy the size of the paper should be nine inches by six, or with sides of proportionate length. Double the paper as in Fig. 1 : turn up the corners *a a*, until they meet at *b*, when the paper will look as in Fig. 2 ;

PAPER BELLOWS.

turn down the two sides *c*, one to the one side, and the other to the other side, to the dotted line *d d*. Insert the thumb of each hand, and pull out the paper so that it may take the form of Fig. 3;

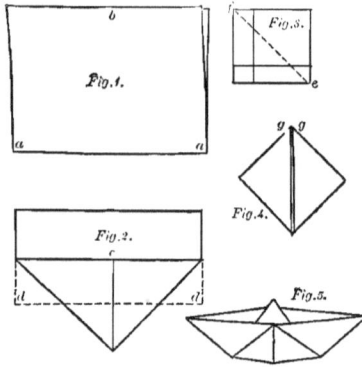

being careful in so doing to arrange neatly the corners *d d* of Fig. 2. Turn up the points marked *e* in Fig. 3, one to the one side, and the other to the other, till they touch the point *f*, folding at the dotted line of the figure. Insert the thumbs again, and pull out the paper to make the form shown in Fig. 4. Lastly, take hold of the paper with the finger and thumb of each hand at the points *g g*, and pull them gently outwards right and left, being careful not to press the inside, and the boat will be complete as in Fig. 5.

PAPER BOAT.

Paper Boxes.—Cut a piece of paper into a square of dimensions according to taste, or according to the size of the box required. As a first attempt a piece of paper about six or eight inches square will be found to be most convenient. Make folds in the paper according to the dotted lines shown in Fig. 1, remembering that in making paper boxes the paper is never to remain folded, except in the last figure, and that the folds are merely to be looked upon as marks for future guidance. Then fold the corners A B C D into the centre, and the folds will show as in Fig. 2. Next fold over and unfold alternately, A to H, B to F, C to I, and D to G, after which the folds should

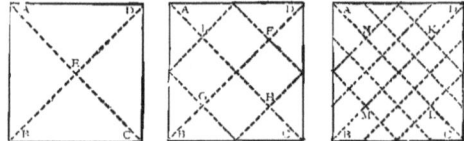

Fig. 1. Fig. 2. Fig. 3.

PAPER BOXES.

appear as in Fig. 3. Then in the same way fold and unfold A to N, B to M, C to L, and D to K, when the dotted lines in Fig. 4 should each be represented by a fold in the paper.

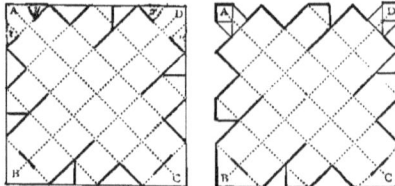

'ig. 4. Fig 5.

PAPER BOXES.

Take a pencil or pen and mark the paper in accordance with the black lines of Fig. 4, and cut with a penknife at all those marks, removing such pieces as will necessarily become detached. Fold and *keep folded* the short sides *x* and *y* of the corners A and D, so that they may pass easily through the slits in the opposite corners B and C. Lastly, and to finish the box, pass the folded corner A through the slit in the corner C, then opening out the folds in order to make the fastening secure; pass the folded corner D through the slit in the corner B in the same way, and at the same time fold in the side that would otherwise overlap.

Paper Chinese Junk.—This paper toy is one of the most complicated and difficult of all the paper toys to make; it requires for its explanation several diagrams, and in the making of it much patience. It takes as long to get into proper shape as it does to form many of the different varieties described under the heading of Magic Fan, and unless great care has been taken throughout there is great chance of the junk turning out but a poor affair after all. In spite of, nay in consequence of, the difficulties, however, it is worth attempting. Take a piece of paper about a foot square, and find its centre by cross folding it corner to corner; fold the four corners into the centre as in Fig. 1, and fold the sides A B and C D to the dotted line E F, so that Fig. 2 will appear. Keep the side of Fig. 2, represented in the diagram, outwards, and double the paper longways to form Fig. 3. Fold both the sides at A B of that figure to the points C D, and the small Fig. 4 will result. Open out again to make Fig. 2, and just under the middle of the outer flaps will be found the four corners of the paper; take two of those corners, one between the finger and thumb of each hand, and pull them out to make the elongated Fig. 5. Double the paper of that figure by the fold A B, so that the two points C D may touch each other back to back. The

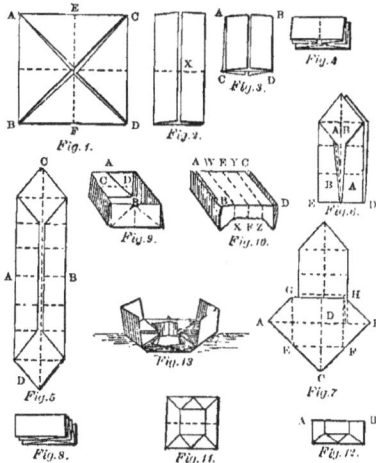

PAPER CHINESE JUNK.

paper now appears as Fig. 6, and it is from here that great care and patience to complete the toy successfully will have to be shown. Take between the forefinger and thumb of each hand the two sides A B, and by pressing them outwards contrive so as to bring the line A C to be parallel with the line C D, and the line B C to the line C E. Into this position the paper must be folded flat, when it will be found to be in the form shown in Fig. 7. Fold the points A B C so that they will all meet evenly at the point D, and then fold the paper so that the line E F will be parallel to and upon G H. Turn the paper over, and treat the reverse side in exactly the same manner. Upon the exactness with which these Figs. 6 and 7 are dealt with depends the success of the endeavour, and if properly done the folding, when completed, should leave the paper as shown in the accompanying Fig. 8.

Insert the fingers then between the folds in that part, which will readily be found, where the paper may be easily pulled outwards right to left, when it will take a box form with overhanging flaps, as shown in Fig. 9. Place the two thumbs boldly on the tops of the two sides marked A and B, and press them firmly down to the table, making the folds inwards, as shown in the dotted line C D. Fig. 10 appears upon the box (Fig. 9) being then turned upside down; fold the line A B so as to produce the fold W X, and press the paper firmly down; fold the line C D to produce the fold Y Z, and again press firmly down. Turn the paper, and it should be fairly represented by Fig. 11. Double the paper outwards by the dotted line, and it will appear like Fig. 12. The test of accuracy in performance now appears. Take the points A and B of Fig. 12 between the forefinger and thumb of each hand, and pull carefully, slowly, and steadily outwards, forcing nothing; if thoroughly made the junk will come quite readily, and will appear bottom uppermost. Turn it over, and raise up the pieces of paper which will be found inside at either end of the boat to do duty as backs to the seats, and all is finished, and should appear as shown in Fig. 13.

In endeavouring to make this toy, keep well in mind that old, old couplet, that the elders are so fond of quoting to the youngsters for their encouragement and edification—

> " If at first you don't succeed,
> Try, try, try again."

Paper Dart.—The Paper Dart is one of the easiest made of the paper toys, and when made will last some time, if put only to its legitimate use. It is best made of a piece of good stout paper, which should be cut so that it is at least half as long again as it is broad. Double the paper lengthways, and make the fold *x z*, as shown in the accompanying figure, opening out the paper again; then turn up the two corners to meet at the points *a a*, and next turn the points *b b* to the point *c* in the same figure, when the paper should appear as indicated by the dotted lines in the figure. Again fold the paper, and retain it folded at the line *x z*; fold down the outside edges so that they are parallel with that fold, and open out the wings so made, and the dart is complete. To throw it, hold the paper on the line *x z* between the thumb and forefinger, take the necessary aim, and cast the dart; its motion through the air will be found to be accompanied with a graceful curve, and to make an accurate aim allowance must be made for the curve. Boys sometimes amuse themselves by fighting sham battles with toys of this description.

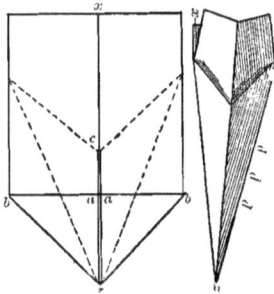

PAPER DART.

Paper Hat (Pyramidal).—The Pyramidal Paper Hat is to be made, so far as its initial stages are concerned, in just the same way as the manufacture of the Paper Boat is proceeded with, and which is fully described in its proper place. The size of the paper out of which the hat is to be made must be decided by the size of the hat required. To make it, proceed as in the manufacture of the Paper Boat, and when the paper is in the form represented by the dotted line in Fig. 2, illustrating that toy, stop short, and turn in the corners of the paper corresponding with the dotted line in the figure, and the Paper Hat will be finished.

PAPER HAT.

Paper Parachute.—To make a toy paper parachute, take a square piece of tissue or other light paper, and fold it from corner to corner into a triangular shape; fold it again from corner to corner. and again a third time fold it in the same way, and then double it so as to give it the appearance shown by Fig. 1 in the accompanying diagram. Cut with a sharp penknife through all the folds of the paper, shown by the dotted lines, and pierce a hole at the point marked A quite through; then, when the paper is opened out, it will be found to be as shown in Fig. 2. Fasten threads, all of which are to be of the same length, through each hole;

bring the loose ends of the thread to a point, fasten them there together, and attach to them a piece of cardboard or folded paper as ballast. The whole toy will then be complete, as shown in Fig. 3. If the parachute be then taken into the open air, and when a good breeze is blowing, the air will soon catch under the toy and carry it up to a considerable height. In the absence, however, of a wind, it requires some dexterity to set the parachute off successfully, and it may be much aided by the use of an arrow and a common bow. A small hole is cut in the top of the paper, in which the point of an arrow is inserted and fixed to the end by a little paste or gum. The ends of the thread should then be tied at about half-way down the shaft of the arrow, and, when complete, it will have very much the appearance of a closed parasol (see Fig. 4). If the arrow is then placed on the string of the bow and shot into the air, the parachute will on coming down open out and sail away gracefully, and more or less swiftly according to the current of air into which it may be propelled from the bow.

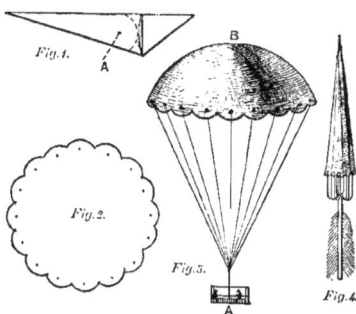

PAPER PARACHUTE.

Paper Purses.—Paper Purses are somewhat complicated in their manufacture, and when made are not the most serviceable of receptacles for money. As an exercise of ingenuity and care in the making they are worth attempting. Cut a piece of paper, tolerably soft and pliable, into a square, fold it into three equal parts, and when so folded again fold three times (Fig. 1); the paper now should again take the square shape, but much reduced in size. Take the paper when so folded between the forefinger and thumb of each hand, and pinch it into the star-like form shown in Fig. 3. Then open out the paper as at the beginning, being careful not to press it flat, but to retain clearly the marks of all the folds, which should be impressed as shown in Fig. 2. Catch the opposite corners at the points *a* and *b* and *c* and *d* respectively between the fingers and thumb of each hand, and by gently twisting and screwing the paper, humour it so that the folds will arrange themselves and leave the paper as shown in Fig. 4. Turning now to Fig. 4, fold the point *a* to the point *b*, *c* to *d*, and *e* to *f*, which should then leave the paper as shown in the Fig. 5. Insert the point *g* of that figure into an opening that will be found between the points *h* and *i*, and the purse, properly closed, is complete.

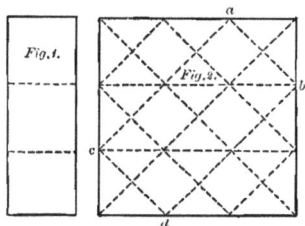

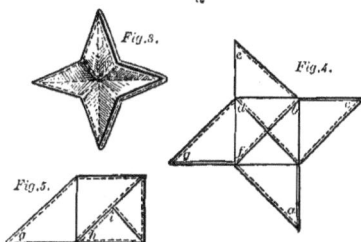

PAPER PURSES.

The chief of the paper toys made by merely folding the paper have now been described; there are doubtless many other simple ones that need no description, and it has not been considered advisable to enter into the details as to the many simple toys that may be cut out of stiff paper or cardboard. Light-fingeredness, guided by a very small quantity of ingenuity and inventive powers, will suggest the uses to which cardboard may be put as an in-door amusement in the manufacture of sundry toys and other miniature articles. A very nice suite of doll's furniture may be readily cut out of pieces of stiff cardboard.

PARLOUR BOWLS.

This is an interesting game, adapted for any number of persons, and in principle is very similar to the game of Bowls, as described at large among the Lawn Games. The balls are, of course, very different in size to those used out of doors, and are made and adapted for in-door play. Each player is provided with two balls of the same colour, which he bowls towards a jack or die, the jack being placed at the side of the room opposite to that from which the players are stationed. The players decide the order in which they play, and then each one alternately bowls one of the balls towards the jack, and he who succeeds in placing his bowl nearest to the jack wins the game. When the players are more than three they may be divided into opposing sides, and it is then legitimate to play so as to knock an opponent's bowl away from, or a partner's bowl near to, the jack; scores should then be calculated after each round, according to the various distances that the bowls are from the jack. The game described in this book as German Balls is sometimes also known as Parlour Bowls.

PARLOUR CROQUET.

There are three versions of the lawn game of Croquet that are played in-doors, and are known as Carpet Croquet, Parlour Croquet, and Table Croquet respectively. These are all recently introduced games, and are deservedly popular. The mallets, balls, and arches are made of different sizes and shapes according to the game; they are all more or less similar to those used in the out-door game, and may be obtained, with the necessary rules, which are only adaptations of the rules of the out-door game, of the toy-dealers. Each version of the game may be played by eight or any less number of players. The peculiarity of *Carpet Croquet* is, as its name implies, that it is played on the carpet, and the hoops used are fitted into flat metal stands, so that the balls roll over the stand without hindrance. *Parlour Croquet* is played on a mahogany board lined with cloth, and which is made level by means of adjusting-screws fitted underneath. *Table Croquet* is played on an ordinary dining-table, and with the other materials for playing the game are supplied cloth cushions to place round the edge of the table to prevent the balls from rolling off.

PARLOUR QUOITS.

An in-door game played with rings very similar to those used in the lawn game of Quoits is known variously as Parlour Quoits, Annulette, and Ringolette. The game bears but slight resemblance to the out-door game of Quoits, but is more nearly allied to that of Skip or Ring the Nail, which will be found among the Minor Out-door Games.

The game is one of skill, and is adapted for any number of players; it is played on a round board, or sometimes on an inclined plane. On the board nine pins, pegs, standards, or skittles of various colours, or differently numbered, are fixed, and the game consists in the players endeavouring to throw each of nine rings—coloured or numbered, as the case may be, to correspond with the pegs—on to its appropriate peg, each player counting towards game the number of the rings successfully thrown upon the proper pegs. Penalties are incurred by lodging a ring on any peg other than that to which it is proper. Each player alternately should throw all the nine rings.

PATCHESI, OR HOMEWARD BOUND.

This is one of the many varieties of the Race Game, described more in detail under that heading further on ; the game of Homeward Bound differing in that it should be played by four persons instead of an indefinite number, as in the ordinary race game.

Each player is provided with dice and dice-box, or, if it be preferred, the game may be played with a common numbered teetotum. The board on which the game is played is arranged as shown in the accompanying diagram, and three pieces or men are allotted to each player, who—according to the throws of the dice, and subject to such laws as have been laid down, or as may be laid down, by the players—has to move these men first along the two outer rows of squares up towards home, returning the reverse way, and ultimately up the centre row to home. Whoever first reaches home wins the game.

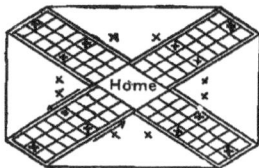

PATCHESI.

PEGASUS IN FLIGHT.

This is one of the few balancing toys which may be readily made, and which will afford much amusement to all, and wonder to those who have not taken the pains to understand the principle on which it is constructed. It furnishes a solution of a popular mechanical problem or paradox, viz., *"how to prevent a body, having a tendency to fall by its own weight, from falling, by adding to its weight on the same side on which its tendency is to fall."*

The Pegasus in Flight when complete is fairly represented in the accompanying illustration. It should be made out of a small toy figure or a horse in which the centre of gravity is found in, or very near to, the middle of the body. The wings, which are merely added for the sake of adornment, and to make the toy resemble in appearance the fabled charger after which it is named,

PEGASUS IN FLIGHT.

should be attached to the figure at a point just behind the shoulders; the wings should be of equal weight and so adjusted as to keep the balance of the figure true. They may, however, if desired, be entirely dispensed with, or any other addition, according to fancy, may be put upon the horse's back. A wire bent to a curve, and to the end of which a small leaden ball has first to be attached, is to be fastened to the middle of the under part of the horse. Upon the hind feet of the horse being then set at rest on the edge of a table, and in such a position that the leaden ball is beneath the edge of the table, the animal may be made to rock to and fro without any fear of its being upset, and the longer the wire, provided only the proper curve is given to it, the longer will be the distance that the toy will sway upwards and downwards. This toy is also sometimes known by the name of the Mechanical Bucephalus, but it should then be made minus the wings, as is also the case when it is simply exhibited under the still more common description of the Prancing Horse.

PITH DANCER.

The Pith Dancer is a very pleasing dancing toy, and possesses the great merit of being easily made. It is a little figure made of cork, pith, or some other equally light material. At one end of the substance cut out a head and bust, and at the other end stick in four hog's bristles of equal length, so that the figure will stand erect thereon. To make the figure effective in appearance, paint the face, put a little cap on the head, add a pair of arms, and dress it in a cloak which may be made of some light stuff like tissue paper. When the figure is completely made and equipped, stand it on the bristles upon the sounding board of a piano, and play some brisk and lively tune. The vibration of the piano will then make the figure dance with much spirit, vivacity, and originality.

PRANCING HORSE.

See " Pegasus in Flight."

PROPHET.

The Prophet, or Sybil, as it is sometimes called, is a toy affording much amusement and diversion for the youngsters during the winter evenings. By its aid fortunes may be told and predictions as to circumstances of the future made with great confidence, for if the predictions should happen by any chance not to come true, the whole responsibility can be readily cast upon the Prophet. The toy is easily made, and by varying the table of prognostications the Prophet's opinion on an almost endless variety of topics may be taken.

To make the toy, cut a piece of pasteboard, a few inches in diameter, into a circle, and ornament the edges with some pieces of fancy paper. Then mark on the white surface of the pasteboard twenty equal divisions, by means of lines radiating from the centre, and within each division place a number ranging in order from one to twenty. The figure of the Prophet should be made so that he has a venerable and sedate appearance, should be clothed in a robe reaching to his feet, and he should hold in one hand a small rod for a wand, which is to be made pointing downwards. The figure may perhaps be purchased, but it is better that it should be made, as it may then be more readily adapted to the taste or fancy, and it can be easily cut out of wood, cork, cardboard, or some other material. It will add much to the general appearance if the Prophet be supplied with a loose white beard.

When the card and figure are finished, the card is to be mounted upon a small wooden stand, through the centre of which a steel wire is placed, and the figure of the Prophet is to be fixed on the wire in such a manner that it may revolve freely.

The next thing to be done is to draw up a table of prognostications, which must equal in number the spaces marked upon the cardboard disc. This may be

THE PROPHET, OR SYBIL.

done in many ways. Sometimes the company present may be requested each to supply a set, or to supply alternately one of a set; or it is better, perhaps, that he who is about to show off the oracle should previously have supplied himself with several sets, one of which, of course, must only be used at a time. The sets should be so arranged that each one is complete in itself, and the various prognostications in a set should bear some sort of relation one to the other.

When all is ready, the performer should desire some one of the company to have his or her fortune told. The prognostications to be used are then to be handed to some other person, and the figure of the Prophet is to be set spinning, and according to the number of the division at which the wand of the Prophet points when it comes to a standstill, so, according to the prognostication bearing the corresponding number, may the fortune of the inquirer be expected to be.

The following prognostications may either be used, or may serve as models upon which tables can be drawn up :—

1.—At the end of a changeful life, wealth.
2.—Early and prosperous marriage.
3.—Great success at school.
4.—A speedy and important journey.
5.—Will spend much time from home.
6.—Hours of pleasure, followed by years of care.
7.—May expect to be thwarted.
8.—Will have invitations to numerous parties.
9.—All work and no play makes Jack a dull boy.
10.—Travels by land, and voyages by sea.
11.—Many changes will be your lot.
12.—It will be your misfortune, not your fault.
13.—A hearty playmate and a constant friend.
14.—Changes in love at an early date.
15.—A long life and a merry one.
16.—Fears from a rival, but success ultimately will be yours.
17.—Beware of a false friend.
18.—Bright and cheerful in youth.
19.—Unhappy ere long, but the sunshine will follow in the end.
20.—Your present sweetheart will not be your mate.

It will be seen that some of the above are very definite, but it is generally advisable that the prognostications should be vague, and capable of more than one interpretation, or the infallibility of the Prophet is likely not to be implicitly believed in. The Prophet is a very useful toy to introduce into a drawing-room entertainment for children, especially where he is not known (and he is not frequently met with) ; a few sets of prognostications will prove a source of a good half-hour's fun with a lot of inquiring youngsters.

PUFF AND DART.

The game of Puff and Dart is very similar to that already described under the heading of " Dart and Target," and is one of the games included by many under the more general description of Drawing-room Archery. The dart is made in the same manner, but of a smaller size, as is the dart used in the game of Dart and Target, but instead of being thrown from the hand towards the target as in that game, it is in this propelled through a small tube by a puff of the breath. The target is precisely similar to the target used in the sister game.

Darts shot by the breath through tubes are favourite weapons of offence among certain Indian tribes ; they, however, first dip the tip of the dart in some poisonous substance, and then send it at the enemy. It is a deadly weapon, and the tribes using it are very skilful both in their aim and in the force with which the weapon is directed.

PUSH PIN.

The game of Push Pin is certainly a game that does not require a vast amount of ingenuity or intelligence to indulge in with success. It is very contemptuously described in Strutt's " Sports and Pastimes " in the following language :—" Push Pin is a very silly sport, being nothing more than simply pushing one pin across another." But as this description is somewhat vague, it is well to enlarge a little on the simple, but yet to many amusing and interesting, game of Push Pin.

The game is usually played by two players only, and each player puts down on the table one, two, three, or more pins, as may be decided upon. At starting the pins are to be placed in couples, head to head, one pin of each couple being placed by each player. Each player then alternately pushes his pin with his finger-nail, endeavouring to push it across his opponent's pin, and should he succeed both pins become his, but if he fail his opponent plays. The push is not to be a continued push, but a sort of a shove with the finger-nail, by bending it on the table and letting it fly up to hit the pin in the required direction.

PUZZLE-WIT.

See " Magic Fan."

QUINTAIN.

The Quintain is another balancing toy, very ingenious in construction. which, although it may be made at home, will be found somewhat difficult of construction. One of the leading toy-makers thus describes its manufacture :—" Carve the bust of a man with a ferocious face ; on the face gum a Turkish beard and moustaches ; let one arm be extended, half bent, holding a wooden scimitar, and the other bear a shield, adorned with an opening, crescent-shaped, in which hangs a little bell. Load the base of the figure with lead, and poise it on a pin, on which it shall so freely revolve as to move at a touch, even so slight as that of a feather. Now, whoever, trying to make the bell ring with his finger, does not thrust at it very quickly, the figure. turning round, will deal him a smart blow on the forefinger knuckle with the sabre."

The principle on which the Revolving Ring or the Revolving Image works is precisely similar to that of the Quintain.

QUINTAIN.

QUIZ.

See " Bandilor."

RACE GAME.

The Race Game is an interesting round parlour game, which may be indulged in by any number of players up to twelve. It has seen many imitations and modifications of it brought into use. and the games of the University Boat Race and the National Volunteers may be instanced as two specimens of more than ordinary interest ; the first of these, however, can only be played by two persons at a time.

The Race Game proper is played on a board, and is subject to rules supplied with the board and the other materials for the game. The board is marked into divisions, and at certain distances obstacles. such as fences, hurdles. and ditches are placed, for the horses participating in the race to clear. The players having determined the order of playing, each one selects his horse, and places it at the starting-point. Dice and dice-box, or a numbered teetotum, are used, to denote the number of divisions the player's horse is entitled to pass over, but should that number land the horse in any one of the brooks or ditches, or upon the fences or hurdles, the throw of the dice, or, as the case may be, the spin of the teetotum, does not count, and the horse waits for another chance of a move when his player's turn next comes round. Each player alternately takes his chance of moving. The rules by which the game is governed vary considerably, and may be modified in any way agreeable to all the players. The following are given merely as specimen rules, as they are the substance of those most frequently supplied with the game :—

RACE GAME.

1.—When the stakes are agreed upon and the pool made, each member must select his horse, and then enter him at the starting-point.

2.—Each member throws, or spins, for choice of move ; the highest number claims the first move, and the others according to the number thrown.

3.—The horse that reaches the winning-post first gains the pool, the second horse saving his stakes.

4.—Steeple or hurdle races can be played by placing fences and hurdles along the course, and any player throwing a number that would place his horse so that he does not clear the fence forfeits his throw, and waits his next turn.

Although the game is made more interesting when played with the materials supplied at the toy-shops, these are by no means indispensable. Any ordinary board, or school slate, may be marked into the necessary course and divisions over which the horses are to travel ; a few horses may be readily cut out of some stiff card-board, and a common teetotum will furnish all the materials absolutely needed for the game. It will be found that the game, so arranged for, will well repay any little trouble taken in manufacturing and obtaining the necessary horses and race-course.

RACQUETS (DRAWING-ROOM).

The game of Drawing-room Racquets is an adaptation of the old-fashioned play of Cup and Ball, so far as is possible, to the game of Racquets played within doors, and in a more or less limited space. The game is usually played by three persons, but the number is immaterial, and may be increased according to the size of the room in which it is played. The game consists in throwing the ball or balls from one cup held by one player to some other cup held by some other player. It is best that the balls should be passed round to the different players in order.

REVOLVING RING.

A ring or a small figure may be so constructed and arranged as to be easily balanced on the top of one of the fingers. Take a piece of wood and cut it into the form of a ring, or get a small wooden ring that is perfectly round ; fasten to it two oar-shaped pieces of wood about double the length of the diameter of the ring ; balance the ring when so furnished on the point of a pin, and then, if the balancing has been properly arranged, upon the head of the pin being placed upon the tip of the forefinger the ring may be made to revolve quickly, and at the same time retain its balance, by blowing, at first gently, and then with more force, upon the oar-shaped appendages attached to the ring.

A small figure may be worked in the same manner by cutting a piece of wood to a point, and carving the opposite end into the form of the head and shoulders of a man ; the pair of oars should be attached in the place of arms, and then, if care to make the point of the wood exactly in its centre has been taken, the figure will stand upright on the tip of the finger, and by blowing he may be made to revolve in a most amusing manner. The Revolving Figure is a more amusing toy than the Revolving Ring; but in that it requires so much more nicety and delicacy of handling to get the proper balance, it is not so easily made.

There is a capital game known by the name of " Revolving Ring," adapted for either out-door or in-door games. It is played with variously coloured balls, which are thrown at rings similarly coloured. The rings are fitted to a board, and in such a way that with the slightest touch on the rims they revolve. The object of the game is to throw the six balls through the revolving rings, the players taking their stand from the board at some specified distance. Each successful throw counts three ; and when a ball is thrown through the ring of the same colour the player scores six.

RINGOLETTE.

See " Parlour Quoits."

RING THE BULL.

This is a game very similar to but somewhat more simple than that of Parlour Quoits. It also is a game of skill. It is played upon a wooden block, in which are inserted a number of long iron pins, on which the player has to throw rings provided for that purpose. The players score according to the number of rings that are so thrown as to encircle a pin.

ROYAL STAR.

The materials for this game are a large star with eight long rays, each one of which is painted some different colour; and eight wooden balls painted to correspond with the colours of the rays of the star. The rays of the star are not fixtures, but their bases are merely slipped into grooves in the body of the star, so that they can be easily knocked out with the balls.

To play the game, each player alternately takes all the eight balls, and standing away from the star at a certain specified distance throws the balls at the star, endeavouring by that means to knock out the rays. If a player should succeed in striking out a ray of the same colour as the ball, two points are scored, but if the ball and the ray knocked out are not of the same colour, one point only is scored. If in any throw the star is altogether missed, three points are to be deducted. When the first player has thrown the eight balls, such rays as may have been knocked out are replaced, and the next player takes the balls and commences the game, and so on until all have had a chance. It is well that a curtain or screen should be arranged behind the star to stop the balls.

ROYAL STAR.

SCHIMMEL.

The game of Schimmel, or, as it is generally known, of Bell and Hammer, is a most amusing round game of German origin. The materials for playing the game are comparatively inexpensive. and as some of them can be prepared by any ordinarily clever lad—and all lads are clever—there is no reason why this game should not, were it but better known, attain much more popularity than it seems to be favoured with.

The materials required are—

1.—Five small cards, on each of which are drawn or painted one of the following figures : On one card a white horse, on another an inn, on the third a bell, on the fourth a hammer, on the fifth a bell and a hammer.

2.—Eight wood, bone, or ivory cubes of the size of dice, marked on one side only, six of which are numbered respectively with the numerals 1, 2, 3, 4, 5, and 6 ; the other two cubes being marked, the one with a bell, and the other with a hammer.

3.—A dice box with which to throw the cubes.

4.—A hammer for knocking down the cards to their respective purchasers, which are disposed of by auction, as set forth hereafter.

5.—A bag of counters.

The game may be played by an unlimited number of players, the more the better, it being especially advisable that at least seven should join in the game. The mode of procedure is as follows :—One of the players is to be selected as cashier, and to him has to be entrusted the bag of counters. A considerable number of these should be equally divided among all the players, and if it is desired they may be taken to represent value. Nuts make good substitutes for counters, as to those players not yet troubled with indigestion they possess in themselves a certain value, especially if it be understood that all winnings may be retained (or eaten).

A pool has to be formed, into which each player pays twelve counters. It is then the duty of the cashier to sell by auction to the highest bidders the five cards, the produce of which also is paid into the pool. Each player is at liberty to purchase as many of the cards

THE MATERIALS FOR SCHIMMEL.

as he may be inclined, and, moreover, he is not bound to pay for all, but is at liberty to take credit for a certain portion of his purchases if they exceed the number of counters originally dealt out to him; only payment of the debt so incurred must be considered as a first charge on subsequent winnings. The cards will, by experience at the game, be found to be of various values; but the number of counters to be paid for each is determined by the speculative natures of the players, and it, indeed, often happens that those players who invest in no cards at all are at the end of the game the richest in the matter of wealth as reckoned by counters. The respective values of the cards are as follows :—The white horse ranks first, and immediately

after him comes the inn. the cards representing respectively the bell and the hammer are of about equal value, and come next, while that representing both the bell and the hammer is lowest in the scale, and is worth just half that at which either of the two cards on which are painted the single figures is valued.

The cubes are then to be thrown by the players alternately, their order having been previously arranged. it being always allowed, however, that the possessors of cards take precedence over the other players, and over each other, according to the relative values of their cards. It should be stated rather that each player alternately is entitled to a throw of the cubes or dice, for any player is at liberty to sell his throw to any other player inclined to speculate therein. When the cubes are thrown and show uppermost all blanks, all the players have to pay one counter each to the holder of the white horse, and he again pays one to the holder of the inn. If the cubes turn up with the bell or the hammer, or with the bell and the hammer, the holder or holders of these cards pay one counter to the white horse. When the bell, hammer, or bell and hammer are thrown accompanied with numbers, the amount of the numbers thrown has to be paid in counters to the holder or holders of the cards out of the pool; if numbers are thrown unaccompanied with either bell or hammer, or bell and hammer, the thrower of the cubes receives from pool the number of counters indicated by the cubes.

It is when the pool is becoming exhausted that advantages accrue to the holder of the inn, and this indeed is usually found to be a very speculative holding. If any player in his throw shows numbers combined greater than the number of counters remaining in the pool, he receives nothing from pool, but pays to the holder of the inn the difference between the number of counters remaining and the number indicated by the cubes; for example, if five counters are remaining in pool, and seven are shown uppermost on the thrown cubes, the player who threw the cubes pays two counters to the holder of the inn, and leaves the five counters in the pool. So on the play proceeds, until some figure is thrown which, clearing the pool, concludes the game.

After the holder of the inn card begins to receive payment, should all blanks be thrown, the players throwing the cubes pay nothing; but instead, the holder of the white horse pays one counter to the holder of the inn; should the bell or hammer, or bell and hammer be thrown with the blanks, the holder or holders of the card or cards indicated each pays one to the holder of the inn. If numbers are thrown accompanying the bell, &c., the holder of that card pays to the inn the number thrown in excess of the number of counters remaining in the pool.

SHOVEL BOARD.

The game of Shovel Board was once a very important national pastime, and was much played among fashionable people. Master Slender, in "The Merry Wives of Windsor," makes a reference to the game. from which it would appear that Shovel Board was in Shakspere's time both popular and fashionable.

The game was formerly played upon a long, low table that usually stood in the large hall of a gentleman's house, but was soon adapted to smaller tables, and was indeed frequently played on the floor, the necessary limits being chalked out on the bricks. The following description of the game will be found applicable, whether it be played on the floor or on the orthodox table or board. it being premised that the space marked out on the floor should be about twenty-five or thirty feet in length and three feet in breadth, a space corresponding with the size of an ancient Shovel Board.

The tables on which the game is now played vary somewhat in length, but are usually three feet to three and a half feet wide. At one end of the table a line is drawn parallel with the edge, and three or four inches from it; at four feet distance another line is made over which it is necessary for the weight to pass when shoved or thrown. The players stand at the end of the table, opposite to the two lines above mentioned, each having four flat metal weights, which they alternately shove from them one at a time. The object of the play is to give sufficient impetus to the weight to carry it beyond the mark nearest to the opposite edge of the table, but so as to keep it on the table. If the weight is shoved so that it hangs over the edge without falling, three are counted towards game; if between the line and edge, without hanging over, two are scored; if on the line one only is credited

SHOVEL BOARD.

to the player. The game is usually eleven when two play, but when more than two are jointly concerned that number should be increased.

Those weights that glance off the side of the table, that do not pass the first line, or that fall off the table at the opposite edge, it will be seen do not score. It is sometimes allowed that all weights passing the first, or four-foot line, score one, instead of making it incumbent that the second line should be reached.

The following description of the game, which differs somewhat from the above, appears in the "English Cyclopædia":—"The origin of the game Shuffle, or Shovel Board, is doubtful; it has been practised for many generations . . . and has lately been largely introduced into America. . . . The board, or alley, is thirty feet long by twenty inches wide, perfectly level, like a billiard table, and constructed of some wood which will not warp. Before commencing to play, it is sprinkled with fine sand, and five inches from each end a line is drawn across the board, parallel with the ends. Eight weights or pieces are required, divided into two sets of four each, and marked with distinctive features. The game is played by four people, two against two, one on either side standing at each end of the board. Twenty-one points have to be scored to win a game; each piece which lies over or inside the line, at the end of a round being ' in,' and scoring two points in favour of the side to which it belongs, whilst a piece partly projecting over the end of the board scores three points. Should no piece be ' in ' at the end of a round, that nearest the line counts as one point, and a piece lying exactly on the line is counted ' in.' The players ' shuffle ' alternately from each end of the board, the great object of each competitor being to ' *shuffle* ' his own piece in, or drive his opponent's off the board."

SKITTLE CANNONADE.

The game of Skittle Cannonade, or Indian Skittle Pool, is a capital game for boys. It is in its higher development played on an ordinary billiard-table, but a bagatelle board will answer all the purpose, or it may even be played on a common dining-table, provided that round its edges are placed such cushions as are supplied with a Table Croquet set.

Two white balls, one red, and one blue ball are used in the game, and five small skittles are placed in the centre of the board or table. The skittles are of different values, and are numbered as follows (as shown in the accompanying plan). The first opposite to the baulk is one, that to the right two, that opposite to the first, three, the one opposite to the second, four, and the centre skittle, five. The points are made by knocking down the skittles, as shown hereafter, each skittle knocked down counting points according to its number. In commencing to play, the red ball is placed as in the

PLAN OF SKITTLE CANNONADE.

● 3

● 4   ● 5   ● 2

● 1

ordinary cannon game of billiards, the blue one beneath it, and the two white balls are retained for the two players who play first. The white balls should be played with alternately by the players, and no score is made except from a cannon, that is, the ball struck with the cue must hit some other ball before the skittle is knocked down; but it does not then matter by which ball the skittle or skittles are knocked down. The first player is bound to strike the red ball, and the second player the blue ball, but afterwards either ball may be struck at. A ball being knocked off the table, or into a pocket when a billiard-table is used, destroys all the points made by the stroke, and if the ball knocked off is either the red or blue ball it must be again placed as in starting the game. The skittles are replaced after every stroke, if necessary. Thirty-one points, neither more nor less, win the game; any one scoring beyond that number is dead and out of the game; or the survivor from amongst all the players wins the game if no one player scores the exact thirty-one required. Any player knocking down the four outside skittles leaving only the centre one standing, wins the game, having made what is technically called "the royal." After each win a new game is started.

The player who first reaches either twenty-nine or thirty points has the right to stop scoring on his declaring to do so, and any point which he may subsequently make counts to the advantage or disadvantage, as the case may be, of the previous player. This right to stop scoring can only be exercised by one player in each game, and if he who first reaches the required number of points refuses to exercise that right, it passes to the next who attains the required number, and so on.

There is also another version of the game of Skittle Cannonade played on a board specially prepared, and the result of which depends entirely upon chance. A teetotum, as in the game of Cannonade, is used instead of balls and a cue, or sometimes a top is made to do duty for the teetotum. Nine specially-made skittles are used, each of which is placed on a spot inscribed with a number. When the skittles are placed, the top or teetotum is smartly spun at one corner of the board by each player alternately, and the scores are made according to the numbers which are laid bare by the skittles being knocked off them. The great point in the game is to give the top or teetotum a smart jerk when spinning it, so as to make it retain its power of movement as long as possible. This description of the game is far inferior to the version described above, but the whole of the materials form a pretty toy, and much amusement for the youngsters is to be obtained from the game.

SLATE GAMES.

There are a few simple slate games which have been in the past, and no doubt will be in the future, the means of affording innocent amusement to many a youngster. They are none of them very elaborate, are usually intended for only two players, and are best grouped together under the one general heading of Slate Games. The first to be described is the game known as

Birds, Beasts, and Fishes.—Two boys take their slates, and each one writes down the first and last letters of the name of some bird, beast, or fish, first stating from which category the name is selected, and puts a cross for each of the intermediate letters. For example, A elects to write down the name of a beast, and marks on his slate as follows—Hxxxe; B will perhaps select a fish, and mark on his slate Gxxxxxn; they then exchange slates, and each tries to guess the name of the beast or fish indicated, and fills up the blanks accordingly. It is evident that those indicated above are respectively Horse and Gudgeon.

French and English.—A slate should be divided into three divisions, the top and bottom divisions each having a small compartment marked off therein, as shown in the annexed diagram. One of the two end divisions should be allotted to the

English and the other to the French, and marks put therein to represent the soldiers of the respective nations. Each player having provided himself with a well-sharpened pencil, the game is played as follows :—The players decide the order of play, and he first selected, being supposed to be English, places the point of his pencil at the spot marked in the smaller compartment of the English division of the slate, draws it quickly across the slate in the direction of the opposing army. The pencil will, of course, leave a line marking its track, and all the men of the opposite side, through which the track passes, count as dead. Each player plays alternately, and he wins who first kills all the men on the opposite side. The track of the pencil must be rapidly made, and must be either straight or curved; any track in which there is an angle does not count. Sometimes the players turn their heads or close their eyes when making the track.

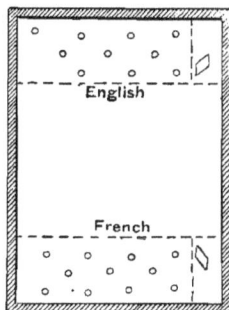

Noughts and Crosses, or Tit-Tat-To.—This game, when played out of school-hours, should be wound up with the following rhyme by him who wins the game :—

> Tit-Tat-To, my last go ;
> Three jolly butchers, all of a row.

"When played out of school?" some readers will say. Yes; this qualification is necessary, for it is to be feared and deprecated that this game, as well as that of "Birds, Beasts, and Fishes," is frequently played in school-hours, to while away the weary time that ought to be devoted to the solution of arithmetical or algebraical problems. These slate games are undoubtedly little boys' games, but many are the big boys who indulge in them surreptitiously, if not openly.

The game of Tit-Tat-To is played on a figure, similar to the annexed, made on an ordinary slate. The players alternately mark in the figure—the one a cross, and the other a nought; he who first obtains a row either horizontally, perpendicularly, or diagonally wins the game, and calls "the three jolly butchers, all of a row." The object of each of the players is equally to obtain such a row, and to prevent his opponent from obtaining one.

X	O	X
O	O	X
X	X	O

NOUGHTS AND CROSSES.

SPILLIKINS OR SPELICANS..

The game of Spelicans is similar to that of "Jerk-Straws." The spelicans are a number of thin pieces of ivory or bone, cut into odd and various shapes—some like saws, some like spears, some like hooks, &c. Each spelican is inscribed with a number, the lowest being 5 and the highest 40. The spelicans are taken up in the hand of any one of the players, except by him who plays first, and dropped upon the table in a heap; the other player or players, as the case may be, then alternately endeavour to remove a spelican from the heap either with the fingers, or by the aid of two small hooks provided for the purpose, without in the slightest degree disturbing any other spelican. At the end of the game each player adds up the numbers marked on the spelicans he has captured, and he who can show the highest number wins. Sometimes, instead of each player alternately trying to remove one spelican, it is allowed for one player to continue removing spelicans one by one until more than one spelican is disturbed in the same try, when the play passes as before.

SQUAILS.

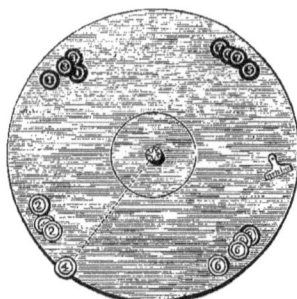

SQUAILS.

In some places the game of Squails bears the name of Trails. It is an amusing round game, which can be played on any ordinary table by two or more players of an even number—not, however, exceeding eight. Each player is furnished with an equal number of coloured wooden pieces or discs, which are called squails, and these the player has to place at the edge of the table, half over the edge, and strike them with the open palm of the hand towards a small medal placed in the centre.

The players should be divided into sides, and one from each side should alternately strike a squail towards the medal. An imaginary circle should be drawn round the central medal, into which, if it is knocked out during the play, it must be replaced. The object of the game is to secure for one's own side the largest number of squails near to the central medal, and to obtain that it is legitimate not only to shove one's own squail towards the centre, but also to knock an opponent's squail away or a partner's squail near to the medal.

The game of Squails, for a year or two after its introduction, seemed in a fair way to rank among the most popular round table games, but it soon died out and is now but little played. It deserves, however, much more notice than it usually receives, and we would recommend it as a great improvement on most of the elaborate toy games that are patronised so extensively. A set of squails costs but a trifling sum.

SQUEAKER.

The Squeaker is an instrument with which it is generally supposed that the peculiar squeak of Punch, in the Punch and Judy show, is produced. To make it, get two little pieces of tin, each about an inch long, and half an inch broad, and bend them slightly inwards.

STEADY TAR.

Now wind a piece of tape round the pieces of tin when placed together, and fasten the whole together with thread. Blow through the instrument, and by the vibration of the central piece of tape a peculiar squeaking sound will be produced.

Another very simple squeaker is made by placing the two thumbs together alongside of each other, and laying as tightly as possible in the hollow between the thumbs a blade of common grass. If the piece of grass is then blown upon, the same horrible squeaking noise will be produced.

STEADY TAR.

The Steady Tar is another toy of the balancing order, several of which have already been described. To make this toy, stick a needle into a cork, and place the cork, needle upwards, tightly into a bottle. Carve the figure of a sailor—any other figure will answer equally well—out of light wood, cork, or pith, and mount him on a hard wood ball. (See figure in the illustration.) Through the centre of this ball run a wire, which must be bent, as in the woodcut, into a half circle, and to either end of which a small leaden weight or bullet of equal weight must be attached. If the hard wood ball is then placed on the needle sticking out of the cork in the bottle, the figure may be spun round, and tipped in any direction; if properly made it will always recover its erect and steady position.

SUMMER ICE.*

This is a capital new in-door game, founded on the celebrated Scottish game of Curling. The materials for the game are made and supplied by some of the toy manufacturers; but the game, which, although founded on

SUMMER ICE.

Curling, has also some resemblance to Shovel Board, may be played on any ordinary table with a plain surface. The materials as supplied consist of a long mahogany folding board, at one end of which is a circle, and sixteen flat weights. It is the object of the players to hurl the weights along the board to reach the circle at the other end. After the players have delivered their weights, that side which has the greater number of stones lying nearest to the tee or mark counts one for each weight so lying. Thus, if side A has two weights nearer than any belonging to side B, the former would count two to their score.

SYBIL.

See " Prophet."

TABLE CROQUET.

See " Parlour Croquet."

TARGETTA.

TARGETTA.

The game of Targetta is a drawing-room game, which is played on a target somewhat resembling a pedestal fire-screen, and similar to the illustration annexed. In the oval central part of the target are fixed a number of pins which are retained in their places by

* This game has been registered by Mr. Cremer, of 210, Regent Street, as has also the following one called "Targetta."

means of springs that are dislodged immediately upon the pins being struck. The pins are thrown at by a ball attached by a long string or cord to the top of the target, and scores are made according to the number of the pins dislodged.

TEETOTUM.

The Teetotum is a kind of top or whirligig that is spun round by twisting the upper part between the thumb and finger. It is usually of a hexagon or octagon shape, but sometimes it is four-sided only, and may be easily made by cutting a piece of wood of an inch or thereabouts in diameter, and a third of an inch in thickness, into the required shape. A stick run through the middle and fixed makes it complete, and the result is a useful rough and homely teetotum.

Originally teetotums had four sides only, which were respectively marked with the letters T, H, N, and P, signifying Take all, Take half, Nothing, and Put in again to pool. The toys, as now improved, are made with more sides, and are variously numbered. In many of the toy games a teetotum is used in place of dice, but simple teetotum games are played with nuts or some such things for stakes. There are otherwise no special games for the teetotum; it is mostly used in various race and other games of chance.

TEETOTUM.

TIT-TAT-TO.

See " Slate Games."

TOURNAMENT.

This is another new round game, a development of and improvement upon some old friends. It is played on a circular mahogany board. A number of tops, teetotums, or champions of different colours are spun in the centre of the board by different players, and these tops are apt to strike and knock each other about. The player whose top dies nearest the centre of the board wins the game. The game may be played on an ordinary tray, or even on a table if desired.

TRAILS.

See " Squails."

TROUBLE WIT.

See " Magic Fan."

WONDERFUL TRUMPET.

The wonderful trumpet is a very simple toy, and to those who like practical joking, affords amusement, except to the one against whom the joke is made. Get a tube made of tin, wood, or cardboard, a piece of cork, and the hollow part of a quill. Cut a slice about half an inch in thickness off the cork, and place it about half-way down the tube, as at *a b* in Fig. 1 in the illustration. Next cut a second slice from the cork, making notches round its edge, and a hole in the centre through which to pass the quill. When this is done fix it at the points *c d*, contriving so that the quill will extend about two-thirds of the way down the upper compartment of the tube. Instead of closing up the compartment *e* with a piece of cork at the point *c d*. wood, tin. or cardboard may be used, it only being necessary that a number of small notches or holes should

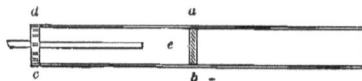

Fig. 1 —SECTION OF WONDERFUL TRUMPET.

be cut in the material used. The trumpet is then complete, and should be represented by Fig. 2.

The following is the use to which it is put:—Place flour, or some harmless dust or powder, in the compartment of the tube marked *e*, block up as instructed the end at *c d*, hand the trumpet to him against whom the joke is to be directed, and instruct him that by blowing through the end of the quill protruding an effect both marvellous and unexpected will be produced. "Blow hard," say; "the harder the better." If he carries out his instructions the flour or powder will come through the holes or notches at the point *c d*, covering the face of the poor unfortunate victim. Viciousness in the use of this instrument should be sternly condemned—a little flour in a boy's face will not harm him, but great care should be taken to ascertain the effects of the material placed in the tube, as certain powders lodging in a person's eyes might do serious injury. Practical joking is not to be much encouraged, but, practised occasionally, and with fun only for its object, is not to be entirely condemned.

Fig. 2.—WONDERFUL TRUMPET.

In winding up the section on Toy Games and Toy-making, it is appropriate to quote the remarks of some of the jurors of the Great International Exhibition, held in London in 1862, who said in effect, when speaking of toys generally, in setting forth their views on the subject, "that toys should be vivid, innocent, and delightful; fitted to teach children to open their eyes, to compare and to observe, and to make them aware how rich and varied are the phenomena of the fair world into which they have been placed, and how much happiness is to be obtained in it."

The manufacture of children's toys forms a very considerable item in the leading industries of the world. The United Kingdom of Great Britain and Ireland alone imports foreign toys to the amount of upwards of £200,000 annually, and this is entirely in addition to the considerable support given to our extensive home manufacture. Among the miscellaneous toys referred to at the commencement of this section were "Noah's Arks," and much wonder has frequently been expressed at the small sum for which toys of this nature are to be purchased. They are usually the product of the skill of the Germans and the Tyrolese. In the Valley of Grödnerthal, in the Tyrol, where almost every cottage is a carver's workshop, Noah's Ark animals are made in very large quantities from a species of pine. The wood is cut into slabs, of from fifteen inches in diameter by three inches thick, the grain of the wood being in the direction of the thickness. A circular piece, six inches in diameter, is cut out of the centre, leaving a ring four or five inches broad. This ring is turned in a lathe, with chisels and gouges, over every part of the surface, on both sides, and on the inner and outer edges. The curvatures, ridges, &c., are very remarkable, but are perfectly understood by the workmen, and by them only. The outer ridge is then cut up radially into slices, each of which slices presents the outline of some animal on both surfaces, the shaping of the wood in the lathe having been such as to bring about this result. Each separate piece is ultimately brought to completion by hand-carving. One of the museums in Kew Gardens, near London, contains specimens of this singularly ingenious manufacture, in various stages of progress.